EFFECTIVELY LEADING

A Guide for
All Church Leaders

by

Richard Patterson, Ph.D.

EVANGELICAL TRAINING ASSOCIATION
110 Bridge Street • Box 327
Wheaton, Illinois 60189

Unless otherwise noted, Scripture quotations are from the New American Standard Bible, © The Lockman Foundation 1960, 1962, 1963, 1971, 1972, 1973, 1975, and is used by permission.

Cover photo by H. Armstrong Roberts

7 6 5
0 9 8

ISBN: 0-910566-53-4

CONTENTS

INTRODUCTION

Should church leaders strive to be efficient or effective? Peter Drucker, the world-renowned authority in business management, writes in his text *Management: The Effective Executive,* (published by Harper and Row) that efficiency is doing things right, while effectiveness is doing right things. The dictionary supports his distinction. It defines *efficiency* as performing adequately, while *effectiveness* is defined as producing results that accomplish one's purpose.

Effectively Leading: A Guide for All Church Leaders contends that while much of what church leaders do may be efficient (adequately keeps the church operating), they are often ineffective (do not produce results which accomplish their true goals). The term *effective* is even used in the title. Though you, as a church leader, should be efficient in your ministry, the greater priority must be on becoming effective in that ministry. To be effective may mean shifting resources from existing functions, programs, and approaches, that though efficient in performance, are ineffective in accomplishing the church's goals.

The pages that follow give priority to the areas church leaders must face in determining whether current leadership programs, approaches, policies, and functions are, in fact, resource-effective in accomplishing the goals Jesus established for the church. Based on extensive research and consultations with thousands of leaders, the theme of the text is that church leaders be both efficient and effective.

This book is the textbook for the ETA *Effectively Leading: A Guide for All Church Leaders* course. This course is part of the Association's Church Ministries Certificate Program. Complete instructional resources are available for those wishing to teach the course. These materials include a copy of the text, instructor's guide, audio cassette, and a set of masters for making overhead transparencies.

Due to the nature of this content, we at Evangelical Training Association realize there may be those who desire to study this text individually rather than in a classroom setting. Therefore, we will provide information for independent study.

WHAT IS 1
CHURCH
LEADERSHIP?

To understand what the Bible says regarding church leadership, we must first define the church. For if we misunderstand what the church is, our perception of church leadership will be distorted. When we view the church as a religious organization representing God's interests on earth, we will naturally view church leaders as administrators and managers.

Jesus was quick to dispel that distortion when He instructed the disciples that they were not to lead as "those who have authority over them" (administrators and managers) but as "one who serves" (Luke 22:25-27). Jesus was not saying that church leaders shouldn't strive to be good administrators or managers, but that they should not make fulfilling these roles their priority and, thereby, simply reflect what gentiles do.

The church, as presented in the Bible, is both an *organism*—the living body of Christ (1 Cor. 12:13)—and an *organization* (Acts 6:1-6). The church cannot be effective for God and be only one or the other. In fact, such a concept is impossible. For even the simplest of life form organisms have organization or they could not exist.

The definition of the church

The theological term, *ecclesiology*, describes the study of the church. Examining the early portions of the Bible, no evidence of organized religious life is found. Further examination reveals a concept that evolves into organized religious life.

The Old Testament church concept

In the earliest chapters of the Bible, the nearest idea to a church concept was that of the family. In the earliest families, the father acted as the priest and leader (seen in Adam and Noah) and later the role of father expanded to that of patriarch (as seen in Abraham, Isaac, Jacob and his twelve sons). Under Moses, religious life changed and a theocracy (the rule of God) emerged. In a theocracy, God was the chief Ruler, Priest, King, Prophet, and He established His law, tabernacle, and temple. Perhaps the best term to describe such persons who worshipped and obeyed God during this period is simply the *people of God.*

The New Testament reality

In the New Testament, however, the concept of church is definitely developed. The term *ekklesia* is now used to describe an organized group of persons whose intent is to worship and obey God.

Recognize that the church is not an improved Judaism, for it is not pouring "new wine into old wineskins" (Matt. 9:17). Also realize that the church is not the Kingdom, for the Kingdom is larger and represents the saved of all ages. Neither should the church be identified with a single denomination.

The church exists in two senses in the Bible. First, in the universal sense, the church is all who have been reborn of God and baptized into the Body of Christ. And, second, in the local sense, the church includes those in the universal church who have linked themselves together in a specific community.

The functions of the church

The New Testament reveals some thirteen separate functions of the church.[1] As a church, they:
- had a definite doctrinal standard (Acts 2:42; Eph. 2:20).
- met for spiritual fellowship (Acts 2:46).
- united in prayer (Acts 12:12).
- practiced baptism (Acts 2:41).
- observed the Lord's Supper (Acts 2:46).
- kept account of their membership (Acts 2:14,41; 4:4).
- met for public worship (Acts 2:46).
- provided material help for their needy (Acts 6:1-6).
- had church officers (Acts 14:23). At Ephesus, they were elders (Acts 20:17); at Antioch, they were prophets and teachers (Acts 13:1); at Philippi, they were bishops and deacons (Phil. 1:1).
- had stated times for their meetings (John 20:19,20; 1 Cor. 16:2).
- raised money for the Lord's work (1 Cor. 16:1,2).
- regulated church decorum and discipline (1 Cor. 14:34; Matt. 18:17).
- sent letters of commendation to other churches (Acts 18:24-28).

The government of the church

From these functional beginnings, followers of Christ have interpreted three different approaches to church government which they see as taught in the Bible. These three approaches are: episcopal, presbyterian, and congregational.

Episcopal

Those who accept this approach believe the Bible teaches that bishops act as overseers and that there are three offices with administrative authority for the functions of the church. In descending order these are: bishops, presbyters (sometimes called priests), and deacons.

Presbyterian

This approach believes elders rule. Church authority is vested first in a local session, moving upwards in authority to presbytery, synod, and general assembly.

Congregational

In this form, the congregation rules. Each church is autonomous with only Christ as its Head.

Whichever governmental approach your church believes is taught in the Bible, it is the pattern in which you will need to function as a church leader. Examining each approach reveals basic principles of Christian leadership which are common to all. And, as an aspiring church leader, you will need to reflect these qualities regardless of which approach your church uses.

The features of the church

Regardless of denomination, period of history, or geographical part of our world, five identifying features earmark the church for all ages.[2] These five features are: a high view of God, the absolute authority of Scripture, sound doctrine, personal holiness, and spiritual authority.

A high view of God

The true church of the Bible always exhibits a high view of God. He is not "the man upstairs" or some other humanistic drivel. God is the great "I Am," the almighty God of the universe, a God so holy that the early Hebrews would not even speak His name. The purpose of this true church is to glorify and worship Him in all His splendor and might and to communicate this high view of God to its world.

The absolute authority of Scripture

Though its enemies constantly attack the Bible, the true church holds high the unshakable confidence that the Bible is God's revelation to man. And, as such, the Bible is the only source of truth for determining how people should live and what constitutes right and wrong behavior.

Sound doctrine

Of course, these doctrines come only from the authority of Scripture. The true biblical church clearly understands the Bible's teachings regarding people's relationship to God, themselves, and their world. Sound doctrine is the church's essential skeleton. Thus its membership should not only be well trained in such doctrine, but also held accountable to comply with it.

Personal holiness
It should hold true that when a church has a high view of God, trusts in the absolute authority of Scripture, and sound doctrine, that its adherents will practice personal holiness. Unfortunately, that is not always true today. Like the Hebrews of old, it is entirely too easy to err and verbally agree to such high and lofty values but refuse to allow them to alter one's life to that of personal holiness.

Spiritual authority
To complete this biblical picture of the church, it must be wrapped with an understanding of spiritual authority. Christ must be its true Head (Eph. 1:22; 4:15) and its membership must understand that He mediates His rule through the godly leaders He has chosen (1 Thess. 5:12-14; Heb. 13:7,17).

Understanding the church's biblical description provides insight as to the kind of leadership it requires. For example, knowing the five identifying features of the church also means that church leaders' lives should reflect these features. God calls people to become church leaders. They are not elected by popular vote or elevated by the power of persuasion. The people God calls to leadership should embody these five identifying features. This task of leading a church includes not only its pastor, but all those who lead by guiding, directing, and influencing others toward fulfilling the church's goals. This includes those who are elders, deacons, trustees, board members, committee members, directors, superintendents, chairpersons, etc. All of these church leaders also have a responsibility before God to accomplish the cited church functions. Although all leaders are responsible for their unique areas, they are also accountable to God for assuring that all of these church functions are effectively implemented. It is a team effort, though all members play separate roles.

Basic characteristics of church leadership
Again, the definition of church leadership being used here is *all those who exercise influence, guidance, and direction to those in the church toward fulfilling the church's goals.* With this in mind, in order to be effective, each leader needs to be: a person of vision, action, steadfastness, servanthood, and dependence.

Effective church leaders are not born—they are developed. Though the potential for leadership appears to be inherited, to be an effective leader requires that these God-given leadership characteristics be developed. Someone has said that the world is divided into two camps—the followers and the leaders. And if God, in His sovereign design, determined that you are to be a leader, you must develop that divine gift. This is done by focusing upon those basic characteristics that make up the leader that God chooses to use in His church.

In thinking about these leadership characteristics in the Bible, rather than using a number of leaders as examples, it will be simpler to center on only one—Moses. He clearly evidenced the common characteristics that identify each of the leaders God chose to use for His glory. In Moses, then, and as repeatedly manifested in those leaders God champions for us, all five of the following characteristics are embodied.

A person of vision

Moses deeply appreciated the covenant that God had made earlier with Abraham, Isaac, and Jacob. The vision of the promised land sustained Moses throughout his life. His vision also motivated him from within to be that one person God would use to deliver His people from Egypt's cruel oppression. Moreover, it was this vision that enabled Moses to so inspire the Israelites that they were willing to follow his leadership.

Vision is the dissatisfaction for what is, coupled with the imaginative perception of what can be. The cruelty Moses' people had experienced for so many years deeply moved him. This burden contrasted with what he knew God had promised. Thus, vision was born for what could be. This dissatisfaction with current conditions and hunger for what could be is the basis for all vision. It is evidenced in the lives of not only Jesus but also all the others God chose to use in leadership roles for the church.

Time does not change this basic characteristic of being God's leader. As you seek to become a leader in your church, the first ingredient in your makeup must be vision. You must be able to see the current conditions as God sees them—be they in your world, community, church, or family—and not only realize that they could be better but be able to visualize how they could be better. Being God's visionary requires feeling deep concern for the poor conditions around you. It also means being able to imagine how this condition could be better and how to achieve this visionary position.

A person of action

Early in this century, Thomas Edison said that success is 1% inspiration and 99% perspiration. Though it is absolutely essential for church leaders to be visionaries, it is also true that they must be able to put their vision into action. Taking this step, however, will not always be easy.

Looking again at Moses' life illustrates that acting on visions can bring difficulty. Upon seeing the Egyptians' appalling cruelty toward his people, Moses took action by striking down an Egyptian and hiding his body in the sand. This action set the next cycle of events into motion—exile to Midian, the burning bush, and his commission from the Lord. This cycle would eventually lead to the fulfilling of his promised land vision (Exod. 1–4). Moses also acted by organizing the people toward the promised land.

Similarly, just as in Bible times when Joseph's dreams met with severe opposition from his brothers, today's church leaders find similar tension concerning their visions. This is where you must be able to put your vision into action.

A person of steadfastness

Looking at Edison's example again, we learn that he tried and failed many times before finding the right substance to make a filament that would work in his light bulb. During this tedious experimentation someone said to him, "You have failed more than two hundred times, why don't you give up?" Edison replied, "Not at all. I have discovered more than two hundred substances that will not work. I will soon find one that will." Now that is steadfastness!

Moses exhibited steadfastness as well. He had his detractors. They murmured against him, complained of their conditions, and blamed him for nearly all their troubles. But in spite of these trials he never wavered nor moved. God had chosen him to lead His people and he had accepted this task. And he knew that God had promised the vision. Thus, he stood his ground and did not waver.

We can all identify with Moses as we engage in any church leadership role. As Moses' example was one of steadfastness, so you will need an abundant supply of this characteristic as well as you undertake becoming an effective church leader.

Looking at all the leaders God used in biblical, as well as modern times, steadfastness was always important and this characteristic is no less essential for Christian leaders today.

A person of servanthood

The biblical leadership model has also been that of servant leaders rather than people's "bosses." Moses learned that lesson the hard way. In Exodus 18, Moses was putting his vision into action by being the judge of his people. From early morning till late at night, he sat in judgment while they brought every detail of their lives to him for solutions. Moses' father-in-law, Jethro, said, "The thing that you are doing is not good" (v. 17).

Surely, this must have hurt Moses. After all, he was God's chosen leader, the man of action, the one with the vision. Why shouldn't he be the boss? Moses had a three-pronged challenge. The first was that he had more ministry than he could handle.

Secondly, he assumed that God intended to use only him in achieving this vision. The third challenge was to realize that God intended for him to harness the strength of the group. This was servanthood. The solution came when Moses carefully delegated others to share his role. This plan worked and Moses succeeded in achieving his vision's goals.

Thus Moses learned that leadership is not a synonym for lordship. Lordship is not God's design for effective church leaders today either. Perhaps, as a result, we should coin the term "servantship" as contrasted with lordship.

The servant leader model is portrayed continually throughout Scripture. Jesus highlighted this principle and provided the paragon servanthood example when He washed His disciples feet at the table (John 13:1-17). By doing this, Jesus stressed that servanthood was the necessary characteristic for the disciples' leadership. On another occasion, Jesus said that He did not come to be served, but to serve, and give His life as a ransom for many (Mark 10:42-45). And that "servantship" is the model for church leaders of this age.

A person of dependence

At sometime during their ministries, almost all church leaders become "weary in well doing." It is almost inescapable. The vision fades. The actions become fatiguing. The steadfastness is hard to hold. It is then that effective church leaders need to again remember Moses' example. In numerous incidents Moses goes up into the mountain to take his problems and concerns to the Lord. Count the times. You will find it refreshing. One of the most beautiful passages in the Bible is Exodus 33:11 which marks one of these times when Moses sought God. It says, "Thus the Lord used to speak to Moses face to face, just as a man speaks to his friend."

Clearly during these times when the vision faded, when action was wearying, when steadfastness was difficult, Moses depended on his Lord. Moses did this so frequently that the Lord felt the relationship was that of a man speaking to his friend. Though the world is constantly changing, that need for depending on the Lord for sustenance, support, guidance, strength, and courage never will. Depending on the one who has called you, who has given you the vision, who has given you the action plan, who is giving you the steadfastness, who is modeling the servantship, is the final piece of the mosaic that creates the picture of biblical and effective church leaders. As in Moses' example, God intends for us to be in that face-to-face relationship with Him. God desires to be so intimate with us that He can say He speaks to us "as a man to his friend." This is the basic fuel needed to be the effective church leader that God wants you to be.

Summary

Though our world is rapidly changing and the church is having significant difficulty maintaining relevance in such a world, the church's purpose does not change. And since the church's purpose does not change, neither do the characteristics needed in the church leader.[3] It is refreshing to note that when the church is what God designed it to be, and when its leaders are who He asks them to be, the church will always be effective in being the salt and light of its society. That is your task.

Notes

1. Robert L. Saucy, *The Church in God's Program*, p. 98, Chicago: Moody Press, 1972.
2. John F. MacArthur Jr., *The Master's Plan for the Church*, p. 25-29, Chicago: Moody Press, 1991.
3. George Barna, *The Frog in the Kettle*, Ventura, CA: Regal Books, 1990.

For further consideration

1. If the concept of the people of God (known today as the church) encompasses all history, consider the historical importance of your role as leader and the people of God. What are the implications?
2. Since there are five distinctive features of the church, how should they be personalized in the lives of church leaders?
3. Compare the areas you are assigned to supervise as a leader in your church to the list of church functions presented in the chapter. If you do not find your area of responsibility mentioned in the list, which should have priority on your time and energy—the function list or your leadership assignment?
4. Which of the five basic characteristics of church leadership are weak in your life? What can you do to correct them?

Application activities

1. Which of the five basic characteristics of Christian leadership seem to be weak in the existing leadership of your church? What can you likely do to improve that situation?
2. Do a biographical study of a New Testament leader, pointing out the five basic characteristics of Christian leadership.

ACHIEVING BIBLICAL GOALS

It is self-evident that before goals can be reached, they must first be identified. That statement surely is not profound. Yet, much of church ineffectiveness is caused by obscure or displaced goals. An old saying states, "If you don't know where you are going, you will get there every time!" In a world of change where values are crumbling nearly every day, if they are to be effective for the Lord, it is imperative that churches and their leaders have clear goals that are biblically based.

To bring such goal setting into clearer focus, let's review what the Bible says regarding the church's mission.

Biblical mission of the church

The Bible identifies six separate goals to which the church and its leadership must commit their energy. They are each listed below with their accompanying Scripture references and in the order which they should occur.

Glorify God (Rom. 15:6,9; Eph. 1:5,6,12,14,18)

Notice that glorifying God is listed first. Until glorifying God is the primary goal of the church and its leadership, there will always be the potential for significant error. The Scripture does not give priority to building buildings, establishing a television ministry, or other tangential issues, but to glorifying God. Giving God glory must be the driving force behind each decision, effort, and program of the church and its leaders.

Edify itself (Eph. 4:11-16)

Ultimately, it is the Lord, through the ministry of His Spirit, who causes edification. Nonetheless, He does this through church leaders. This does not mean, however, that church members should be passive. Edification is each believer's responsibility. And not only that, all Christians are also accountable to God for edifying their brothers and sisters in

13

Christ. Thus, edification is the chief internal goal of the church. In achieving this goal, the church also glorifies God.

Purify itself (Eph. 5:26,27)

Purity is an area of church life that is in serious disarray today. Rather than focusing upon purifying itself, multitudes of conflicting goals are preoccupying church leaders. In an age of selfishness, when societal values encourage individuality and individual freedom with widening tolerance for all behavior, purity is not a welcome theme. Yet, the Bible says that the church and all believers stand totally pure before God simply because the church is hidden in Christ. This is positional purity.

There is also practical purity. And this must be a daily exercise, not only for all believers, but the leaders of the church as well. Ultimately, of course, only Christ will cleanse His church sufficiently so it can take its place in heaven. Yet, God gives the church a solemn goal of purifying itself—in a practical sense—in the everyday life of its membership.

It is the responsibility of the church and its leaders to provide the setting where this divine purification can work among the membership. Certainly this requires the church and its leaders to submit to God. It also demands both individual and corporate self-discipline. The church which fails to make this an essential goal of its ministry for Christ will not be able to serve Him effectively in its community. It may still be a very effective and prominent organization; but, it cannot be that unique "body" that God uses to lead people to Christ.

Evangelize its world (Matt. 28:19; Mark 16:15)

Some may quarrel with placing this goal so far down the list. Such positioning does not infer evangelism is an inferior goal, however. It only highlights that, in order for the church to effectively evangelize its community, it must first be glorifying God, edifying its membership to maturity in Christ, and purifying itself as true salt and light to this world. Note also that biblical evangelism does not mean that the church's goal is to transform the world. That will not occur until Christ returns. The goal of evangelism is for the church and its leadership to communicate the gospel of Christ to the world. This communication should cause men to acknowledge and glorify God and repent of their sins and accept Christ's substitutionary work.

Restrain and enlighten the world (Matt. 5:13-16)

Distinct from evangelism, the church is exhorted to act as "salt of the earth." It should bring out positive "flavor," or positive features in its world. Further, the church is instructed to be the "light of the world." The church is to be a beacon of light which shows the true way to a world that is in darkness.

The practical implications of this are immense. The church and its leadership must determine how it can most effectively penetrate into the world.

The Scriptures make it clear, however, that the church will never accomplish this goal by separating itself from the world. Since the church finds pleasure in the fellowship of the saints, it will require considerable leadership effort to insure that this goal of evangelism is accomplished.

Promote that which is good (Gal. 6:10)

Though somewhat similar to the previous goal, this one focuses more on individuals both inside and outside the church. This goal calls upon the church to be a positive role model to each person in the world. Scripture never encourages treating men and women outside the church in a harsh and degrading manner. Quite the contrary, the church is instructed to "love its enemies." Similarly, Philippians 1:10 exhorts the church to approve those things which are excellent. This exhortation affects all that we do.

No doubt, other church goals could be cited; but our purpose in listing just these six is to focus heavily upon the essential nature of the church and its responsibility to God, itself, and its world (in that order). The Bible clearly states that the primary focus of church goals are upon Him. Then, only as the church matures in edification, is it competent to work toward goals that are in its world.

Typical goal cycle of the church

Some interesting factors are seen in the studies of churches and their goals. One of these factors is that nearly all churches undergo a life cycle. They begin with a dream. That dream spawns goals. Those goals produce an organizational structure by which the church can accomplish its goals. This results in a positive ministry to its world. Positive ministry means the members primarily minister to the community outside the church. The original dream produces a ministry that has as its goal the meeting of needs in the world outside the church.

This initial positive ministry, however, often degenerates into a negative one. That is, the church's ministry efforts change from being directed toward those outside the church to that of sustaining itself. They begin to focus their energies on maintaining their own organizational structure, boards, committees, programs, etc. The dynamic energy of the church and its leadership turns inward. This trend is quite clear. This inward focus has serious consequences. It often causes members to question the church's goals. This questioning then begins to polarize the membership which leads to despair, unhappiness, and a sense of uselessness. The result eventuates in the death of the church.

Unfortunately, this cycle is repeated frequently all across the world. The situations can be corrected, however. Many churches discover that they are in this vicious cycle and break out of it by creating a fresh dream of ministry. Such a fresh dream, when generated from the grass roots of the church membership, shifts the church away from pursuing this destructive cycle. Dreaming new dreams is a healthy and necessary experience for each church, its leaders, and membership. Without such review and correction, the church is inevitably pursuing a course toward its own demise.

Dreaming such new dreams is exciting. It requires, however, that the church, as a corporate group and as individuals, go back to the Bible. There they rediscover what the church's mission truly is and then begin to meaningfully apply this biblical mission to their own specific group and time. It stresses the unique setting of this church group, the society around it, and the apparent gifts that God has bestowed on its members. As all of this data is blended, meaningful biblical goals for this specific group will surface.

It is in this dream that the cycle will begin once again. This fresh dream will produce fresh goals. These fresh goals will generate fresh organizational structure to achieve these goals. The result will again be positive ministry to its world.

Importance of goal setting

Five components of goal setting are valuable to church leaders.[1] Setting goals is a healthy endeavor for the church for it presupposes goal clarity, promotes total planning, precedes church ministry, predicts organizational control, and presumes accountability.

Presupposes goal clarity

As stated earlier, obscurity of goals is an unfortunate characteristic of many churches today. Thus, the process of establishing goals demands that the group determine what the goals will specifically be. Just thinking through the biblical injunctions of the church's mission along with candidly assessing the qualities and talents of those who make up the church and reviewing the current needs of its surrounding society, is an important therapy for revitalizing the church.

For example, a popular goal churches often propose is that they grow. Yet, carefully reflecting on this goal often reveals that size is not everything. Church growth, while a mark of success in many situations, may not be the primary goal that God chooses for every church. This, however, does not mean that smaller is necessarily better either. It simply means that the church and its leaders need to do their homework concerning what God is saying are appropriate goals for them.

Promotes total planning

Goal setting must be done in the context of the church's total ministry. The church cannot effectively plan goals for its mission program, for example, if it does not do so in the context of its entire ministry.

To help focus on the church's total ministry, the members and their leaders should do what is called a "mental helicopter ride." This is simply a mental exercise where the church's leadership imagines they are in a helicopter hovering over their church's physical plant some five years in the future. While looking down from the helicopter, they should try to visualize their church in five years. What would it be like? How would it function? A fresh vision or dream often results. It is quite revealing how church members can identify with this technique and begin to see how totality of ministry—rather than only one facet—is needed to achieve proper goals.

The second stage is for the church to formulate a package of decisions that will help it get from where it is today to that idealized future. This requires the group to determine what decisions must be made now to get started in that direction, what energies and resources must be committed to that decision, and what requirements will be needed to sustain direction toward achieving their goals.

A good acronym for such decision packages is **SAM**. Each decision which helps achieve their goals must be **Specific**, **Attainable**, and **Measurable**. That is, each step must be so clearly spelled out that the group understands what is required. That step must also be attainable with the time, talent, and resources that are to committed to it. And finally, each step must be measurable in that the group can determine to what extent it is being achieved.

Precedes church ministry

Proper goal setting argues that the church must be willing to assess every action, function, or program it is involved in at the moment. It is "point zero." It is a time when the church and its leadership openly and candidly look at everything they do. This is done to determine the degree to which that factor, program, policy, or effort is moving them toward their stated goals. Some of the questions that should be asked are:

- Is this effort successful? What are the measures of this success?
- Is this meeting today's needs?
- Is this endeavor feasible? Does it demonstrate cost effectiveness (time, energy, and money)?
- Is this manageable? Is it within the parameters of the church leaders' control?

- Is it furthering our stated goals? In what ways can we specify this?
- Is it properly coordinated with our other ministry efforts?

Frequently when churches, under the guidance of their leaders, place every church activity and decision under such scrutiny, a climate ripe for change follows.

Predicts organizational control

As stated earlier in the life cycle of the church, goals determine the organizational structure. Most church organizational structures today are built on a previous generation's dreams and goals. These churches often revere their current structures as their heritage, when, in fact, such structures may well be the basic hindrance to fulfilling their heritage. Organizational structures are no more than tools to use in achieving and implementing goals. They are as expendable as they are practical. Church organizational structures should change as frequently as their goals and conditions. God intends that structures be used to realize our goals but not to be slavishly bound by structures which are no longer effective in realizing those goals.

It is often traumatic for churches and their leaders to consider their organizational structures this way. They have assumed there is some eternal biblical exhortation that originally established their organizational structure, which must be relevant to the present time and kept through all ages. Such is not the case. Clear goal setting places goal achievement primary and then chooses whichever organizational structure will most effectively reach that goal.

Presumes accountability

With disturbing frequency, the Bible projects a day of accountability for everyone. This day of accountability is not diminished because people are believers. This accountability is different for Christians, but a reality nonetheless. God will hold the church and its leadership accountable as well. Passages such as the parable of the talents in Matthew 25, and Paul's exhortations in 1 Corinthians 3:11-15 and Ephesians 5:27, all shed light on the way believers will be held accountable to God.

When setting goals, we need to remember that God will hold everyone accountable for all that they do. This is no less true of the church than each believer. Thus, whenever goals are being established, we must do it with a sense of awe realizing that our performance toward achieving that goal will be part of our meeting with the Head of the church, Jesus Christ.

Hence, all of what we do falls into the "20/80 principle." That is, 20% of what we do produces 80% of the results. While, conversely, 80% of what we spend our time and energy on only produces 20% toward realizing our goals. Thus, church leaders who desire to be effective must be quite cautious about how they spend their time and energies. Easily, that 80% factor can be highlighted and made a priority, later to find that it was only 20% effective in achieving their goals. It is quite easy for churches to get so wrapped up in the activities of the 80% group that, though they may be efficient, they may not be effective.

Another issue must be raised when talking about achieving biblical goals. That is, planning for such goal completion. Dr. Kenneth O. Gangel identifies three principles of planning.
* *Goal achievement will occur in direct ratio to its planning.* All goals have much greater likelihood of completion depending upon the energy spent in planning for its achievement.
* *Planning must increase in specificity as the time for goal achievement approaches.* Though church leaders must engage in long range planning, as the time for goal completion nears, planning must increase in intensity in order for goal completion to be sure.
* *The effort desired must be commensurate with the result desired.* Planning for goal achievement is work. Merely citing goals and then vaguely or carelessly planning for their achievement consigns those goals to incompletion.[2]

Summary
The most serious problem facing the church and its leaders today is the lack of clear goals derived from the Word of God and the harnessing of corporate energies to achieve such goals. Ted Engstrom observes that a major sign of this malady is the large number of church staff, committees, departments, or boards that are organized around what they do rather than what goal they are trying to complete.[3] A definition of a good church leader could be one who guides and develops the activities of others toward the completion of group goals. With such a definition, it is important for all church leaders to realize that they are accountable to God for group goal establishment and completion.

Effective church leaders don't wait for events to happen; they help make them happen. Effective leaders do not assume that goals will be achieved; they insure that they will be achieved.

Notes
1. Richard Patterson, lecture notes for "Revitalization of the Twentieth Century Church," Moody Graduate School course.
2. Kenneth O. Gangel, *Leadership for Church Education*, p. 222-223, Chicago: Moody Press, 1970.
3. Ted W. Engstrom, *The Making of a Christian Leader*, Introduction, Grand Rapids, MI: Zondervan, 1981.

For further consideration

1. What other goals would you like to add to the list in this chapter? What biblical evidence do you have for such goals? Where would you place your additional goals in priority relationship to those cited?
2. Explore the differences between objectives, aims, and goals. What role should objectives or aims have in your leadership?
3. What is the membership's role in determining group goals?
4. What is the role of church leaders in determining group goals?

Application activities

1. Locate the stated goals of your church (they are probably cited in your church constitution). Compare them with the cited goals of this chapter. What are your conclusions?
2. Identify where your church is in the typical cycle of the church. What evidences can you cite to demonstrate that your assessment is accurate?
3. Develop an action plan where your church's leaders can address the concerns you have raised in activities 1 and 2.

DEVELOPING A MINISTRY TEAM $\boxed{3}$

As a church leader, you are going to need all the help you can get! Repeatedly the Bible exhorts believers to serve the Lord together, rather than individually. Our salvation is a personal experience with the Lord, but our service is to be a group effort. The book of Proverbs often warns us to listen to counselors, "But a wise man is he who listens to counsel" (12:15). If we are to serve the Lord in a team approach, we need to understand what the Bible teaches about team ministry.

The biblical model

The Bible provides many models of teamwork. Although individuals like David and Elijah tend to dominate, careful examination shows that God often used teams to accomplish His goals. For example, David's men killed more giants than he did (1 Chron. 20:4) and Elisha worked more miracles than Elijah.

As in the previous chapter, Moses and the Israelites provides an ideal illustration of the teamwork approach. In Exodus 18, Jethro saw Moses' weariness as he tried to lead thousands of people toward the goal of the promised land. Jethro said, "The thing that you are doing is not good...the task is too heavy for you; you cannot do it alone" (v. 17,18). In other words, Jethro advised Moses to use a team to accomplish the ministry. Moses took Jethro's advice and the results were amazing. Few church leaders will ever experience the success Moses did in properly harnessing the energies of others. Scripture says that Moses actually had to restrain the people from doing any more volunteer work and from bringing their gifts (Exod. 36:5-7). Remembering that Moses served in a setting filled with murmurings (Exod. 16:7) and conflict (17:8), his stunning success, when he harnessed the abilities of others, is a strong lesson for today's church leaders.

Moses thought that being a leader for God meant doing it alone. It took an outsider to see Moses' problem and to show

21

him that leadership in isolation is always a mistake. Moses' motive was not in error, but his method surely was.

Current management texts suggest a five-stage formula for success. The five stages are: all good leadership and management begins with *planning*, eventuates into *organization*, moves to *staffing*, then *directing and coordinating*, and, finally, concludes with *controlling*. Though management literature may use different terms, the principles are the same.

Notice that Moses exhibited these five stages thousands of years before anyone thought about such management principles. In Exodus 18:19, Moses established objectives (planning). Verse 22 mentions that he identified the functions, responsibilities, authorities, and accountabilities (organization). Further, in verse 21, with careful discernment he selected his personnel to satisfy the needed functions (staffing). Verse 20 illustrates how he guided and led their efforts to the cited goals (directed and coordinated). Finally, in verses 23 and 26, Moses oversaw all of their efforts (control) to insure that the goals were met.

Moses was not alone in such team-creating efforts. We see similar team building in Jesus' ministry in the New Testament. Eims observes that, to Jesus, men were His work, not His programs. Therefore, Jesus exercised considerable care in selecting His team. He spent the entire night in prayer before selecting them. This is the principle of *selection*. Eims further points out that Jesus chose His team of disciples to help accomplish His goals, just like Elijah chose Elisha to be his helper. This is the principle of *association*. Finally, Eims cites the principle of *instruction*. To illustrate this principle, he points out that Jesus not only spent time with His disciples doing the everyday work of the ministry, but He spent much time instructing them.[1]

The teamwork model does not stop with Moses or Jesus. In Acts 6, the early church leaders found that expanding their team helped them to better reach their goals. Even Paul had various team members traveling with him on his ministry tours. Undoubtedly, the concept of team leadership is a biblical one.

Today's church leaders should follow this biblical approach rather than the singular leadership model many current well-known personalities have adopted. Paul instructs us frequently that our ministry is not to seek our own interests and needs but those of others (Phil. 2:4). The biblical model is not that of individualism, isolation, nor empire building in the name of God, but that of humbly serving God together. God desires church leaders to *supplement* each other, building on one another's strengths and compensating for other's weaknesses. Also, it is God's design that leaders *encourage* one another by motivating them to fully develop their gifts and abilities. Finally, it is God's plan that church leaders be *accountable* to each other. Perhaps no other single factor caused the amazing growth of the early Methodist Church than being accountable to one another on a weekly basis.

Contextual leadership

A term that best describes biblical leadership is contextual. That is, leadership in a context or setting. Leadership has elements and factors that surround and mold it into a unique effort. There are different styles of leadership. One type is the laissez-faire model, where the leader gives minimum direction and provides maximum freedom to others. Another is the democrative-participative type of leadership where plans and policies become the result of group decisions. Another is the benevolent-autocratic style of leadership. This approach takes on a "father knows best" style of thinking and decides for others according to what the father believes is in their best interest. Finally, there is the autocratic-bureaucratic style. Unfortunately, this style of leadership is often found in Christian organizations. These type leaders are not accountable to anyone who can truly check or challenge their thinking and decisions. Since man is a fallen creature, even when saved, such leadership style will fail in achieving spiritual goals for God.

Contextual leadership depends upon the leader's personality type, the group being supervised, and the setting.

The leader's personality type

Everyone has a personality type that can be identified. This personality type strongly influences their leadership style. Some of these styles are:

- sanguine (outgoing, talkative, but weak-willed and undependable)
- melancholy (gifted and analytical but self-centered and moody)
- choleric (strong-willed and independent but cruel and proud)
- phlegmatic (calm and easy-going but stingy and fearful)

Often personalities are a blend of these four. Although our personality types are what they are, the Spirit of God can help us enhance the positive traits and modify the negative.

Don't assume, however, that the servant leadership model found in Luke 22:27 necessarily prescribes a democratic leadership style. On the contrary, the Greek word used in that verse is *diakonon*. In using this word, Jesus meant that the disciples were to serve in a humble manner. They were singled-out leaders. They were chosen by God. Jesus said they had power, authority, commission to heal, raise from the dead, cleanse and drive out demons (see Matt. 10). Servant leaders are those that serve best, and they do it in humility.

The group being supervised

Contextual leadership is participatory; that is, it depends upon the context of the group. Acts 6 illustrates this well. As the early church grew, the disciples needed help in caring for its needs. So they chose from among themselves others who could share the ministry tasks. Notice that it was the leaders who sought the participation (v. 3) and appointed the team (v. 5), it was not a democratic election. For they were most accountable to God for achieving the goals.

Performance leadership is also contextual leadership. We found that illustration in Moses. He was called to lead the Israelites from Egypt. Though he felt inferior, slow of speech and tongue, he also realized that he had a goal for which he was accountable. Moses realized that leadership is making things happen. Reviewing Exodus 36 confirms that Moses was successful in making things happen.

The setting

What is the best leadership style? As was pointed out earlier, it is the leadership style that best suits your personality (as modified by the Spirit of God), the needs of the group you are guiding, but it also depends on the setting under which you serve. This, of course, means that your leadership style must change as these factors or elements change. Your leadership style is simply a strategy for effectiveness. That is, "what style should I use which will reflect the models of the Bible and most likely accomplish the goals (both of people and programs) we have chosen?" It will always be contextual leadership.

Distinguishing between managers & leaders

Many management consultants believe that some persons make better managers while others make better leaders. People usually have gifts in one of the two areas, but not likely in both. This is not to say, however, that one is inferior to the other. It simply means that each gift is different and must be considered when developing your team and assigning tasks. Following are some of the distinguishing factors:

- the leader designs; the manager develops the design.
- the leader creates; the manager makes the creation happen.
- the leader is the entrepreneur; the manager is the doer.
- the leader pursues the future; the manager maintains the present.
- the leader uses people; the manager uses the system.
- the leader infringes upon structure; the manager builds structure.
- the leader takes risks; the manager seeks stability.
- the leader depends upon the trust of people; the manager depends upon the control of people.

There may be other distinctions, but these contrasts depict the differences sufficiently to show that church conflict can occur when a manager type is expected to perform leadership tasks and vice versa. It is also true that when there is more than one leader type in the church, conflicts often result. Further, churches can flounder when there is no leader type or when there is no manager to complement the leader. You will find yourself predominantly in one category or the other. Recognize, however, that to successfully achieve goals you will have to have your counterpart, be it either leader or manager.

The people with whom you serve

To build their teams, church leaders must understand what the Bible says about people. It is clear that each person was created in the image of God. What is not clear to many are peoples' capabilities in the eyes of God. Though many shudder when the term perfection is mentioned, it is a biblical one that must be considered when studying peoples' capabilities. The proper way to understand such a word is to allow the Bible to interpret itself. The concept of perfection can be interpreted in three ways—positional, prophetical, and progressive.

Positional perfection (Heb. 10:14) declares that believers are positionally perfect as Christ takes their place before God.

Prophetic perfection involves the believers' experience as they, upon death, are ushered into the arms of their loving Savior (Phil. 3:11,12; 1 John 3:2; 1 Cor. 15).

Progressive perfection (2 Cor. 7:1) declares that all believers can progressively increase in spiritual perfection as they mature in the faith. In fact, this perfection is the *purpose of Scripture* (2 Tim. 3:16,17), the *plan for the ministry* (Eph. 4:11,12) and the *premise for all teaching* (Col. 1:28).

What this simply means is leaders must hold a high view of every person's capability. This includes those they are charged with leading as well as those on their ministry teams.

These capable persons have all been given a personality that is both inherited and societally-determined and have been given spiritual gifts that are divinely issued. Each is a unique creation that is designed to be functional in the Body of Christ. Failure to fully utilize such persons is to frustrate God's divine plan for leaders.

Building your team

Unique leaders need unique ministry teams. This is true whether you are a pastor, superintendent, staff leader, department head, chairperson, or whatever church leadership role you fulfill. This does not mean that you are only "one of the pack" and that everything should be decided by reaching a consensus. That is not the biblical model. It does mean that everyone is essential to accomplish effective goals. You need the differing personalities and viewpoints. You need others to be tolerant in the pace of change. You also need the ability to analyze the differing perspectives and insights and interaction with others as a context for you to decide and exercise clear direction.

Therefore, three elements must be part of your plan when building your ministry team. These are: selecting, motivating, and supporting.

Selecting

Selecting the right people for their teams was critical to Moses' and Jesus' success. So also it will be essential in building your team. Selecting the right people is the most challenging task.[2] Since nearly one-third of the population moves each year, coupled with sickness, and other personal issues, recruiting team members will be a year-round process.

The Bible does not support selecting team members simply because they are willing. This certainly was not the case with either Moses or Jesus. Issuing public invitations for people to volunteer does not require that they be automatically selected as team members. The selection process requires getting to know the volunteer's spiritual background and personal history. Investigating people in this way should also provide you with a sense of how effective the person will be in helping you accomplish the church's goals. This process must be carried out before asking anyone to join your team.

The process of selection should also include deciding before-hand what roles you desire the prospective team members to fulfill. Often this is accomplished by designing carefully formulated job descriptions. Job descriptions include what qualifications team members should have (knowledge, lifestyle guidelines, evidences of spiritual maturity, etc). It also clearly outlines responsibilities and expectations of the ministry tasks. An effective way to evaluate prospective team members is to watch them in as many settings as possible. Are they exhibiting the qualities that they need to join your team as staff members, teachers, elders, superintendents, committee members, etc.? Further, you need to decide what pledges you are willing to make to them as you consider recruiting them.

When you become convinced that the prospective team member could be the right fit for the task, you will want to spend time in prayer, just as Jesus did, asking for God's guidance in approaching this person. Recruiting the wrong person for your team can cause considerable conflict and injury to you and your team and ultimately prevent realizing group goals. Proceed slowly and cautiously through your selection process, always remembering that leadership goals are accomplished by having qualified people in the right positions on your team.

Motivating

The motivational process begins with enlisting the team member. As the team leader, the way you present the ministry task often determines how motivated the person will be to accept and fulfill it. Thus, when approaching the person, always stress the importance of the task and how uniquely qualified they are to fulfill it. Diminishing the task only makes it seem unimportant and unfulfilling and usually determines that the recruit will only devote minimal energy to it. A good principle to follow in recruiting is that workers usually perform at the "level at which they were recruited." Present the task in such a way that the recruit sees it as important enough to devote whatever is necessary to join your team.

Stressing the spiritual growth opportunities is the next step. Emphasize the impact their service will have for Christ. People want to have their lives count. They want their ministry to make a difference in their own as well as others' lives.

Next, you will want to explain the responsibilities. Assuming that newly recruited team members will automatically understand what will be expected of them is a serious mistake. Further, don't minimize the expectations fearing that prospective team members will not accept your offer because they might feel it will require too much time or effort. Present all expectations clearly. Often poorly communicated expectations later lead to team conflicts.

Promising the benefits should be your next step. Outline the rewards for fulfilling the ministry task. These may include the blessing of God that comes from knowing that they are serving Christ and perhaps impacting others' lives for Him, in-service training, adequate materials or supplies, support staff, and any of the resources under your control that will make their task more successful and fulfilling. In the case of professional team members, benefits would also include such things as salary, office space, and vacations.

Once the above steps are completed, allow sufficient time for personal decision-making. In the initial interview or offer to the prospective team member, do not press for a decision. Allow time for the Spirit of God to confirm whether an effective match has been made. Conclude the interview with prayer, allowing your prospective team member to pray, as well as praying yourself. This mutual process shows the prospective team member that you intend to share in the achievement of the group's goals.

Prospective team members are motivated more by recognition, satisfaction, and sensing they are meaningfully contributing toward fulfilling agreed-upon goals than by titles, rewards, or office space. Thus, as a church leader, emphasize those motivational elements the prospective team members will value most.

Supporting

Once team members are enlisted, your task has just begun. If you are to enjoy a fruitful relationship, it is necessary for you to support them as their leader. This support encompasses a wide range of resources, from your personal pledge to pray for them to providing all the people and materials necessary to do a good job.

In the midst of this is the team members' vital need to sense fulfillment and satisfaction. Recognition and affirmation—noting their accomplishments privately and publicly—will help achieve this. It is important that team members feel that their contribution is so vital that the group could not achieve its goals without them. This brings fulfillment and satisfaction to your team. As church leaders you will need to explore avenues which make this sense of fulfillment and satisfaction clearly focused to every member.

Use whatever meetings that are necessary to stimulate and enrich this support. Wherever possible, pair up new team members with more seasoned workers who can act as mentors. Provide additional encouragement by suggesting further training through correspondence courses, evening school programs, group field trips to similar ministries, regional conventions or conferences, and good reading materials.

Summary

Every church leader needs workers who are committed to helping accomplish the church's goals. From the earliest Bible times through today, the leaders who accomplished the most for God used the team ministry model. The team model requires the leader to coordinate the qualities of others to best achieve the church's goals while helping them to grow spiritually and achieve personal fulfillment. It does not infer, however, that all team members share equal authority. Whatever the setting, size, scope, visibility, or the titles of the team members, to accomplish all that God calls you to be and do as a church leader, will be done better by developing an effective team.

Notes

1. Leroy Eims, *The Lost Art of Disciple Making*, p. 29-36, Grand Rapids: Zondervan/NavPress, 1978.
2. Leonard E. Wedel, *Building and Maintaining a Church Staff*, Nashville: Broadman Press, 1966.

For further consideration

1. Contemplate what might have happened if Moses had not heeded his father-in-law's advice.
2. Was Jesus' model of selection, association, and instruction limited to His style of leadership? Why?

3. From your understanding of the Bible, cite some of the liabilities of team leadership.
4. Identify several leaders in the Bible that did not use a team model. What were their strengths and weaknesses? Why?

Application activities

1. Specify four features of your church leadership that will help team members feel a sense of fulfillment and satisfaction.
2. Personally explore your own approach to leadership to determine whether you are the manager or leader type. What are the implications?
3. Examine whether you are a dominant sanguine, melancholy, choleric, or phlegmatic personality type. What are the negative features of that dominant personality you need to ask the Spirit of God to help you change.
4. Create an imaginary ministry team for yourself. What would the other members look like (sex, race, age, etc.), how many would there be, and what personality traits and manager/leader types would they represent?

4 USING YOUR MINISTRY TEAM

Having created your ministry team, as a church leader, the next step is to begin to deploy them. Looking again at Moses' example in Exodus 18 illustrates this step well. In an earlier chapter we learned that Moses realized he had more ministry than time and energy to accomplish it. To counteract this problem he carefully selected others to join his ministry team and to share the tasks. Jethro gave him excellent instruction when he told Moses to choose "able men who fear God, men of truth, those who hate dishonest gain" (v. 21).

It was more than selecting his ministry team, however, that made Moses successful. It was also the way he assigned the specific tasks to each member. And what made the difference was his skill in matching people's capabilities and potentials to the proper tasks (v. 21,22). Though all team members had basic qualities (loyal, enthusiastic, and capable), each also had unique skills and abilities that Moses identified and then linked with a specific task. He chose some to be leaders of thousands and others to be leaders of tens.

Though Moses deployed these team members into a wide array of ministry tasks, he remained the person who was accountable before God (v. 26) and was still responsible for monitoring his team's effectiveness and making the tough and ultimate decisions. Nevertheless, he had multiplied the scope of his leadership energies for God far wider than if he had tried to do it alone. Always remember that what is most important to God is not so much what we can do for Him, but what He can do through us.

Augustine, an early church theologian, is reported to have said, "Without God, we cannot; without us, God will not." In that same fashion we add, "Without a team, we cannot; without us, others will not." Hence, to accomplish church goals, delegation is necessary.

Interestingly, much of the secular futurist literature argues for a similar approach to accomplishing goals. For example, Naisbett, in his popular book, *Megatrends*, reports that people are moving from centralization to decentralization. In addition, Tom Clancy's work, *In Search of Excellence*, analyzes successful leadership and cites that one of the features of all of these leaders was that they were productive through other people.

Three components of delegation

Delegating is not simply asking team members to do the busy work you dislike, it means doing only what you can do best and allowing your team to do the rest. If delegation is to be effective, however, three components must be in balance— responsibility, authority, and accountability. If these three components are not in harmony, discord among team members will occur and your leadership will not be as effective as it could be.

A good model for all three components is found in Matthew 10 and Mark 6 where Jesus carefully described the *responsibilities* for each of His disciples (Matt. 10:1-23). In His descriptions He also gave them specific *authority* by which they could fulfill these responsibilities (Matt. 10:1). Jesus did not, however, leave His team members with only two of the leadership components intact, He also made them *accountable* to Him (Mark 6:31,32).

Responsibility

In this formula, the term responsibility means whatever obligation or task the leader delegates to the team member. This responsibility must be clearly defined both to the team member and the leader. It is best that this be written. Job descriptions are one facet of responsibility. The principle is, if the leader expects the team member to perform a responsibility, it should be clearly written and explained to be sure it is understood.

The most frequent cause for ministry conflicts is poorly-communicated responsibilities. The usual pattern is the leader assumes that the team member understands a task. Yet the team member, in reality, has no idea what is expected. Then, when the team member fails to do what is expected, it always produces tension and conflict between the leader and the team member. All responsibilities, regardless of how small, should be clearly written and discussed between the leader and the team member. Also, to avoid intruding on others' territories, be sure other team members understand all that they need to know.

Authority

With responsibility must come authority. All that is needed, however, is sufficient authority to insure that the responsibility can be accomplished. This authority, termed power in management literature, is legitimate and necessary if the leader is to accomplish this responsibility through the team member. Often church leaders assign responsibilities yet fail to provide the team member with sufficient authority to fulfill the task.

This type of authority is usually referred to as positional power. That is, in the organization, this team member is given sufficient organizational power to satisfy the assigned responsibility. It is delegated power from the leader. Thus, the leader must first have this power in order to delegate it to a team member. In the church, many mistakenly believe that all power has evil origins. It is the abuse of that power, however, that is evil. Jesus said that, upon His resurrection, He would grant power to His followers so they could carry out their assigned responsibilities (Acts 1:8). Therefore, delegated power must be in balance with the scope and type of responsibility involved.

Accountability

Of the three components of delegation, accountability is most frequently abused in the church. A distorted view of this concept rampant in the church today is that a person should only be accountable to God, not his colleagues. They say that since they are doing God's work, they are accountable only to Him. Their argument, however, has a serious flaw. Although it is true that everyone is ultimately accountable only to God, it is also true that all leaders have a fallen, sinful nature that is especially vulnerable to abusing power.

Thus, it is necessary to establish proper and adequate checks and balances upon that power. The ideal place to establish this accountability is in the same written format where responsibility and authority are described. If this principle was always followed, many heart-breaking problems in the church could be avoided. This practice is important at all levels of church leadership. If leaders had always set up clear channels of accountability, many of the potential places Satan has robbed them of goal achievement would have been avoided. Such accountability is a strong motivator to godly self-control and Christian conduct.

Delegating to your team

Kenneth O. Gangel, a prominent Christian educator, says that leaders should "get rid of everything you can and do only what remains."[1] This is not assigning only trivial tasks to team members. It is, however, realizing that for leaders to have vision and scope as well as be persons who make things happen, they must retain only those tasks for themselves that they can do most effectively. Leaders will then delegate other tasks to their teams.

Where most leaders struggle with delegation is when they are convinced that if a task is to be done right, they must do it. It is Moses' "me alone" syndrome. D. L. Moody is reported to have said many times in his lifetime, "I'd rather put 100 men to work than do the work of 100 men." This biblical philosophy will serve today's church leaders well.

Yet, as organizations develop and grow, leaders often continue making all decisions themselves. Volunteers, as a result, pursue personal goals while assuming minimal responsibility for any organizational goals.

Why delegate?

When leaders properly delegate, team members feel they have a part in achieving the group's goals, thus achieving such goals becomes personal to them. Delegating helps team members better own these goals. Such involvement in the group's mission and the corporate formulation of group goals also brings increased satisfaction and morale among the team members. Delegating helps the group better understand the church's mission and improves interpersonal relationships. Hence, delegating to ministry team members is a win-win situation for both the leader and the team members.

To leaders, there are additional benefits. Leaders now have decreased their task pressures. With such reduced pressure, they can now broaden their function to their organizations. Rather than becoming overwhelmed with the details of making their ships run, leaders can now concentrate on steering them.

Team members benefit as well. They will be more motivated to accomplish their assigned responsibilities since these tasks are now a part of their lives and values. Further, team members sense fresh opportunities to display, use, and develop their gifts and skills.

When should leaders delegate?

The simple answer to the question of when to delegate is "When someone else could do it." In beginning to carry out the delegation process, leaders need to answer an additional question, "Who on my ministry team can accomplish this task?" Notice that the question isn't "Who could do it better, as well, or poorer than me?" It is, "Who can do it?" If a person on your team can do it, it should be delegated.

Delegation exhibits trust in team members and frees the leader to do only those tasks that team members cannot or aren't qualified to do. Usually the tasks that leaders must do are those that require overall vision of the goals, where they are the only persons who can secure the resources to meet those goals, or where they are the only ones who know how to effectively apply such resources to those goals.

In some cases, only part of the task can be delegated to a team member. That is, sometimes no one team member can do the entire task. Yet, there are members who can do part of it. If so, that part should be delegated. Then perhaps the rest of the task can be delegated to other team members or leaders can complete that part themselves.

Whether the whole or only part of a task has been delegated to the lowest responsible party, the authority necessary to fulfill the task must also be delegated. As was mentioned earlier, an accountability structure must be determined as well.

Gangel lists several key delegation principles that he finds in the Bible. He states that delegation does not come naturally to a leader, is essential for survival, does not reduce the leader's accountability, should be practiced with qualified people, and results in a harmonious organization.

Peter Drucker, the management expert, has often said there are no poor employees, only poor bosses. In the context of this text, we would say there are no poor church workers, only poor church leaders. When tasks are properly delegated to ministry teams, church leadership is improved and better workers are produced. Certainly God intends the church to use biblical delegation principles in order to achieve the goals He has determined for it.

When can tasks be delegated?

In each case, the answer to the question "When can tasks be delegated?" must be, "Only when the tasks to be delegated have been clearly defined." Concepts, themes, or ideas cannot be delegated. If leaders cannot clearly specify the task, determine how much authority is needed to achieve the task, or whether the task is ever accomplished, then there is nothing that can be delegated. A specific written task is basic to any delegation.

Remember, with every delegated task must come the specific authority to fulfill it. And with that authority must also come an explanation of how accountability will be exercised. Successful church leaders plan for all three at the outset of the delegation process. They first determine the specific task, then match the task with the right amount of authority to assure goal completion, and finally, they state the conditions of accountability. And, as was previously stated, at the time the delegation takes place this should all be in writing.

Leaders, however, need to be cautious to delegate only to team members who are ready to accept the tasks. Church leaders need to be careful also not to play favorites when delegating. This will ultimately cause hard feelings among team members. And, finally, leaders should not delegate to someone outside their own ministry teams.

What else should leaders do when delegating?

As the question "What else should leaders do when delegating?" is all encompassing, so the answers are varied.

Leaders should not delegate to team members issues involving discipline, establishing goals, or setting objectives. All three of these areas are leadership responsibilities. Routine details, however, should always be considered for delegation to the most qualified team member. Yet, leaders often desire to use delegation to produce growth and maturity in team members. In these cases, leaders will often choose to delegate problem solving tasks which will likely contribute to that growth.

In delegating, leaders must demonstrate trust and confidence in team members. Leaders should also allow the team members enough freedom to accomplish tasks in their own manner. Leaders may want to establish strategic accountability check points during the tasks, while allowing team members the freedom to make minimal mistakes as goals are being achieved.

Developing the right ministry team is pivotal to leaders' success and sense of satisfaction. Since all teams of church workers are involved in ministry, all members should exhibit ministry qualities. These include: warmth, empathy, genuineness, integrity, caring, listening, availability, bearing with one another, and the ability to encourage. When church leaders have such ministry teams, they will have yoked some of the essential qualities needed to be effective for God.

It is a common expression that the shortest course in human relations is found in the following statements:

- the six most important words are, "I admit I made a mistake."
- the five most important words are, "You did a good job."
- the four most important words are, "What is your opinion?"
- the three most important words are, "If you please."
- the two most important words are, "Thank you."
- the one most important word is, "We."
- the least important word is, "I."

Such a lesson in human relations is also a model for using ministry teams.

Summary

Developing and properly using ministry teams is the key ingredient in being God's leaders in any age. Such teams do not mean that leaders are only one of the members. If God has commissioned and ordained leaders to do great things for Him, He will also give them gifted team members to help accomplish His goals. In Luke 11:9, Jesus said, "...ask, and it shall be given to you; seek, and you shall find; knock, and the door will be opened to you." This principle is true in selecting, enlisting, and training your ministry teams. It is also true in delegating tasks to them.

How leaders use their ministry teams will largely determine how worthy they are in serving God.

Notes
1. Kenneth O. Gangel, *Feeding and Leading*, p. 177-178, Wheaton: Victor Books, 1989.

For further consideration
1. Explore other biblical illustrations where responsibility, authority, and accountability are seen.
2. Research biblical passages for illustrations where there was an imbalance of responsibility, authority, and accountability. What are the implications?
3. Predict what would have been the result if Moses had not balanced all three components of leadership.

Application activities
1. Assess an organizational unit in your church for the use of proper principles of delegation. What are the circumstances? Cite only the facts as you can gather them without raising alarm among the leaders and team members of that unit.
2. Imagine yourself to be an outside church consultant called in to help the above-mentioned organizational unit to achieve its goals. What will be your recommendations regarding delegating tasks?
3. Place yourself five years into the future. As you idealize what you feel God may assign to you, what will your ministry team look like? Who will make up its membership? What tasks do you see now that you feel would be appropriate to delegate to them? How will you make them accountable for achieving the goals?

EFFECTIVELY LEADING MEETINGS   5

Have you ever heard comments like, "A camel is a horse put together by a committee" or "Meetings are boring and a waste of time"? Disdain for meetings and committee work is often valid. But it is not the meetings and committee work themselves that are the problem, it is when they are poorly planned and lack direction.

Looking again at Exodus 18, you remember that Moses was making a serious mistake in trying to do God's work single-handedly. God always intends that His leaders get things done through people. And leading in this manner requires meetings, boards, and committees. For our purposes, boards establish policies for the group; while committees carry out these policies and study, discuss, evaluate, and recommend their findings.

Gangel points out that the central problem with meetings and committees is that, "We have viewed them not as essential service for Jesus Christ, but as a necessary evil to be dispensed with as quickly and painlessly as possible so that service can commence."[1] Learning to properly use meetings, boards, and committees is essential to aspiring church leaders who wish to achieve group goals.

When meetings are necessary

Church leaders often incorrectly assume that they should decide for the group. Lawrence Richards warns church leaders that such is not biblically correct, for that prerogative is given only to Christ. He states, "Our church boards and our pastors have become, at times, decision makers *for* the church, rather than men charged with carrying out the decisions *of* the church." He further observes that it is not who should decide in the church, it is how does Christ *communicate* His decisions to the church.[2] Philippians 2:1-8 illustrates this concept. This passage contends that Christ's design for His church is that it, both individually and corporately, have the same attitude of selflessness, unity of mind, and humility, as He had in His ministry and substitutionary death.

Thus, the question for church leaders is, "How do I insure that it is Christ who is deciding for this church?" Several biblical passages provide an answer.

Church leaders do not act alone

In Acts 1:15-26, an apostolic position needed to be filled. To reach a decision, Peter, as primary leader, guided the others through an election/appointment process. The decision was not Peter's to make; it was Christ's prerogative. The Bible shows that God used a group decision to choose the right person.

Church needs determine when meetings should be called

Acts 4:13-31 demonstrates that church needs determine when meetings should be called. In this passage, the Jewish Council had taken a harsh stand against the infant church and prohibited it from further evangelism efforts. This need prompted a church meeting. The purpose of this meeting was not just fellowship and mutual comfort, but, as a group, to pray for God's guidance in planning their next move.

Meetings are designed to clarify

Acts 11 tells about a time when Peter had gone to Joppa and presented the gospel to Cornelius, a gentile. On this occasion, Cornelius and his household turned to faith in Christ. This incensed the new church. They felt that this was totally against their goals, believing only Jews should be evangelized. A meeting was called to clarify the issue. After Peter explained God's unmistakable call and the Spirit's obvious moving in Cornelius' family, the church did a complete turnaround, realizing that Christ was broadening their goals to include the gentiles.

Meetings are the means to resolve issues

Acts 15 provides the backdrop for demonstrating that, for the New Testament church, meetings should provide a means for resolving issues. In this passage, circumcision was the issue. Interpretations on both sides had severely divided the group. To allow all the parties to openly discuss the issue, a meeting was called. During this open, yet orderly, discussion, James stood up and proposed a solution. This caught the group's attention. It was in this open discussion, after hearing James' proposal, that the early church found the will of Christ.

Three types of meetings

The three reasons to call and hold meetings are—to instruct, to decide, or to solve problems. Notice that one of the purposes is not "because they're scheduled." Meetings should be held only when there is a purpose.

Meetings that instruct

Of the three reasons for holding meetings, church leaders most often overlook instruction. Some instructional purposes for holding meetings are: to inform members of decisions and directions church leaders have already made which affect the whole body of Christ; to hear reports from church boards or committees; to equip, train, or edify church workers to effectively serve Christ.

Since most church workers are extremely busy, they are finding it increasingly difficult to attend all church meetings, programs, activities, and services. Often, church business meetings have a low priority. To try to compensate for this problem, often church leaders, especially Sunday school superintendents, have begun using their regular business meetings for instruction as well.

To fulfill this instructional purpose, ETA created a very convenient set of program resources titled *Training When Meeting.* Sunday school and church educational leaders report that their workers are much more motivated to come to the regular business meetings when they also include helpful instruction in developing their ministry skills and abilities. When church leaders keep the members informed about the workings, direction, and goals of the group, as well as equip them to serve more effectively, they usually have a more cooperative group to lead.

Meetings that decide

Decision meetings are held for such purposes as: dispatching business items; approving proposals within established guidelines and budget; changing current rules; and adding or dropping members.

Information is not the thrust of these meetings. They should be designed to give the wider constituency an opportunity to make group decisions on functional issues and proposals made by the leadership. Of course, this type meeting also allows group members to contribute ideas for consideration as well. Decision meetings should allow all members the freedom to express their viewpoints, but also often require them to submit to the group's decisions.

Meetings that solve problems

When a church faces issues that are not addressed in its by-laws or constitution, often a meeting is called to solve the problem. In some cases, a preliminary meeting of this type is held to explore with the group any possible solutions. In this preliminary problem-solving meeting, the leadership tries to sense the direction of the group, which is acting as a corporate reflection of Christ's body.

More common purposes for this type meeting are resolving personnel conflicts, doctrinal issues, or budget shortfalls. Usually the problem clearly involves the entire group. Often it is an obstacle that is restricting the group from achieving its goals. Thus, the group needs to meet to discuss the issue openly and seek to resolve it. During such meetings, church leaders must be careful to provide the group all the information needed to arrive at a decision. In these situations, often leaders have personal feelings about the issue which makes it difficult for them to remain objective. Irregardless, leaders must not allow their personal feelings to affect the group's ability to come to an intelligent decision.

Depending upon the church's organizational structure, leaders can exercise their viewpoints as individuals. As leaders of the group, however, they must serve the interests of all. Church leaders have two roles to play. They must be true to themselves while remaining impartial to everyone else's interests.

Principles of successful meetings

The ultimate value of meetings is found in the changes they produce in the participants—increased knowledge, attitude, behavior, or habit. According to Wedel, for church leaders to conduct effective meetings, they need to exercise four specific principles: know the rules, have an agenda, always produce records, and depend upon a control structure.[3]

Know the rules

Every group must have rules for its functions if it is to achieve clear goals.[4] In order for all group members to know what these rules are, they should be clearly written and distributed to the membership. In the church setting, these rules can take many forms. The set of goals that the group has formulated should certainly be considered rules for the group. Church constitutions and by-laws are overall rules that should govern all groups. Even the minutes of the group's earlier meetings often become rules that govern later meetings. Whatever form they take, they are the rules which govern the group. Thus, leaders and group members must not only know what these rules are, but must agree to be governed by them.

Frequently, by-laws and constitutions are so outdated that current church members are no longer aware they exist. Such a setting is often the backdrop for leadership failure. If rules are so obscure that group members no longer function by them, they must be revived and then either revised or discarded. If church leaders and their constituency hope to effectively accomplish goals for Christ, they must know and abide by the rules. Otherwise, they may find themselves in the same situation as Old Testament Israel where "everyone did what was right in his own eyes" (Judges 21:25).

If the rules are appropriate and current, church leaders should always have a copy with them at every meeting. If not, leaders should make the adoption or revision of the rules the first order of business. To ensure current rules, churches, boards, and committees should review their by-laws, constitutions, and other documents at least every two years.

Have an agenda

An agenda is a meeting plan. It directs the participants in accomplishing the leader's goals for the meeting. Hence, whoever leads the meeting should set the agenda.

When creating an agenda, meeting leaders should place items in the order of their importance. Usually, agendas follow a traditional format. Typical congregational church meetings, for example, are usually conducted in the following manner. They begin by stating the meeting date, followed by a Bible reading and prayer. Often the first item of business in the meeting is adopting the agenda. Then the business portion continues with reading the minutes of the previous meeting followed by introductory comments or reports of staff members and board chairpersons. The agenda then introduces other items of business beginning with those of greatest importance. Usually groups deal with old business before new topics because it is very easy to get bogged down in trivial issues and run out of time for treating major issues. In order to avoid this problem, sometimes meeting leaders assign a time limit to some agenda items.

Agendas should be distributed to everyone in the group, even those who are unable to attend the meeting. Copies of all agendas should also be given to any boards, committees, and staff members who are affected by the business discussed and decisions which were made at the meeting.

In congregational type meetings, it is best that the pastor or other paid staff member not chair the meeting because, in many cases, they ultimately are charged with carrying out the group's intents and policies. If chairing the meeting cannot be avoided, pastors, or persons in similar positions, must serve two roles: the administrator for the group and the facilitator of the group. The two roles are separate, however, and it will be difficult to effectively accomplish both.

Even if pastors or administrators do not chair the meeting, they should still propose items of business for consideration to be incorporated into the meeting's agenda. Often only pastors or staff administrators are the ones who are aware of the group's needs and, thus, the intents and goals for the meeting. Nonetheless, the chairperson should approve the agenda.

Always produce records

The written records of meetings are called minutes. Often in jest, people say that meetings keep minutes, but waste hours.

When proper minutes are kept, this need not be the case.

It is the leader's responsibility to see that a secretary is appointed or elected by the group and to insure that the secretary is present or must name a substitute. Minutes are simply the record of what takes place in the meeting. Such documents, however, should only record those items that are essential for future reference and function of the group.

After the meeting, the chairperson should review the minutes for accuracy and see that they are distributed to everyone who received an agenda. The secretary should keep a copy of the minutes as a permanent record of the meeting.

Depend upon a control structure

The term control alarms some people. Yet, as illustrated previously, it is a biblical theme. To insure that goals are met, all meeting leaders need to exercise control.[5] Control, however, should not be confused with manipulation. Control involves harnessing the energies and viewpoints of divergent people to focus upon goal completion.

Unfortunately in some situations, control becomes corrupted and takes the form of dictatorial power, a clever use of intimidation in the form of spiritual guilt. In leading meetings, however, control is best carried out in the form of parliamentary procedure.[6] Though the term may seem formal and rigid, they are the rules which allow each member to be heard and help the group to make decisions without confusion. All church leaders who are responsible for conducting meetings should be thoroughly familiar with these procedures.

Parliamentary procedures

It is tragic that many church leaders do not have a grasp of parliamentary procedures. They are rarely found in today's Bible college and seminary courses of study. Hence, they are frequently ignored in church meetings. Yet, they are unmatched in their ability to capture the dynamic of the group toward achieving their goals. Using parliamentary procedures would have kept many church leaders from personal injury and discouragement in their ministries. Using these procedures could have redirected the energies of many participants in church conflicts toward group rather than personal goals.

The following briefly overviews parliamentary procedures. Whoever conducts a meeting must:
- be knowledgeable of parliamentary procedure (though not necessarily an expert);
- establish with the group that such procedure is the only rule that will be followed during the meeting (this must be stated at the beginning of each meeting, often written at the bottom of the agenda);
- have a copy of the adopted parliamentary procedures.

recognizing the chairman

Some will argue such procedure is not necessary among believers, claiming that the New Testament sets no such precedent. Such a claim, however, is only partially correct. The making of motions, etc., is not clearly seen in Scripture. Yet, the principles of good parliamentary procedure are all found in the Bible. Gangel points out that each member:
- has one voice.
- has a responsibility to express his opinion.
- must listen respectfully to all other options.
- must detach himself emotionally from his own ideas.
- must publicly support the group's decision.
- must keep the group processes confidential.[7]

The two basic building blocks of parliamentary procedure are motions and voting.

Motions

A motion is a proposal asking the group to act or to consider some issue. Members can present motions, second motions (express support for another's motion), debate motions, and vote on motions. There are four different types of motions for consideration. They are main motions (they must yield to a motion already on the floor), subsidiary motions (motions which affect the main motion), privileged motions (motions which are urgent, unrelated to the business at hand), and incidental motions (motions which question the procedure being followed). Securing a good book on parliamentary procedure will clarify these four different motions and their use.

In making a motion, members of the meeting must follow a six-step process. First, the member must obtain the floor from the chairperson. Second, the motion is made. Third, they must wait for another to second the motion or it dies for lack of support. Fourth, the chairperson restates the motion for clarity and allows debate of the motion. Fifth, the original member making the motion or someone else may amend the motion. And, sixth, the chairperson calls for a vote on the motion.

Voting

Usually the group's by-laws or constitution determine the method for voting. However, it also can be the prerogative of the chairperson if not previously stated. Five types of voting can be used. They are: 1) *voting by voice* (aye or nay), results determined by the chairperson (however a member may move for an exact count); 2) *voting by a show of hands*, the results determined by the chairperson; 3) *voting by roll call*, each member's name is called and the person answers with his vote; 4) *voting by ballot*, members write their vote on a slip of paper; and 5) *voting by general consent*, when a motion is not likely to be opposed, the chairperson can say, "If there is no objection...", and if members are silent, the vote favors the motion.

Summary

The most effective and biblical way of expressing your leadership in the church will be through people. To do so, you need to become adept at managing people through meetings. This is true of board, committee, and other types of meetings. Church leaders, however, must be cautious about when to use meetings.

Meetings should be called only when they are needed and when they can be used as a tool for achieving the group's goals. Three types of meetings that leaders should use are those that instruct, decide, and solve problems. While using all three different types of meetings, church leaders should be careful to insure that all four principles for successful meetings are evident—know the rules, have an agenda, always produce records, and depend upon a control structure.

Notes

1. Kenneth O. Gangel, *Feeding and Leading*, p. 273.
2. Lawrence O. Richards, *A New Face For The Church*, p. 121, Grand Rapids: Zondervan, 1973.
3. Leonard E. Wedel, *Building and Maintaining a Church Staff*, p. 129ff.
4. Robert R. Thompson and Gerald R. Thompson, *Organizing For Accountability*, Wheaton: Harold Shaw Publishers, 1991.
5. *Robert's Rules of Order*, Tarrytown, NY: Fleming Revell, 1967.
6. E. C. Utter, *Parliamentary Law at a Glance*, Washington, DC: Henry Regnery Co., 1928.
7. Kenneth Gangel, *So You Want To Be A Leader?*, p. 126ff, Camp Hill, PA: Christian Publications, 1973.

For further consideration

1. Explore your Bible to find three additional illustrations of meetings by godly leaders. What principles do you find?
2. What further implications do you see in the biblical injunction that the church have "this attitude in yourselves which was also in Christ Jesus" (Phil. 2:5)? What practical ways should this be seen in your leadership?

Application activities

1. Secure a good text on parliamentary procedures and work out a basic understanding of how you will conduct meetings according to such rules.
2. Create a handout sheet of the types of motions and voting and their use to distribute at the next meeting you conduct.

EVALUATING LEADERSHIP THROUGH WORSHIP AND OUTREACH $\boxed{6}$

In the church today, the poorest areas of performance are that of worship and community outreach. Current church growth and leadership texts cite this growing phenomenon as early warning signs of a deep malady facing the church.[1]

Why link worship and outreach?

Though this linkage is not common, research indicates a direct relationship between these two church functions. In fact, evidence is mounting that indicates a major source of outreach failure in churches today is caused by inadequate worship experience.[2] With increasing frequency, church staff lament that their members have little enthusiasm for outreach ministries. Others observe that today's "meism" culture with its diminishing genuine concern for the plight of others has caused this coolness toward outreach.

Yet, any study of Scripture reveals that people must have a positive vertical relationship to generate a horizontal relationship with others. Without this vital vertical relationship with God, horizontal relationship with society becomes distorted. A proper horizontal relationship with one's society feeds on the vertical relationship with God.

Many biblical examples illustrate this point. For example, as Jesus was introduced to Andrew, a genuine worship experience followed. This experience resulted in Andrew immediately recruiting his brother Peter. The same formula was present when Philip found Jesus and experienced this initial worship, he also sought out his friend Nathaniel and brought him to Jesus (John 1:40-45). In Mark 16:5-7, the same pattern of worship leading to outreach is seen. The angel in the tomb said to the two Marys and Salome, "come and see (worship), then go and tell (outreach)."

45

Why evaluate?

Often people object to evaluating what is done for God. They say that this interferes with the work of the Holy Spirit. This argument states that motive is enough. The outcome has to be left to the Holy Spirit. Frequently, however, this argument is used as license for careless ministry.

Many biblical passages request believers to "test the spirits"—to investigate, evaluate, and analyze what is happening in their lives. This is particularly true of their spiritual lives. The Apostle Paul exhorts believers to, "discern what is best and may be pure and blameless until the day of Christ" (Phil. 1:10 NIV). Again in Romans 2:18 he says, "...approve the things that are essential." How are believers to do this unless they evaluate?

Therefore, it is our spiritual exercise and responsibility before God as believers to evaluate our lives. Consequently we need to adjust those aspects of our lives to conform to His criteria as found in the Bible. Failure to evaluate allows vagueness and nebulousness to govern our lives. Such is the scheme of our soul's enemy, Satan.

Yet, to other believers, evaluating seems to carry a negative image of judging. Jesus' instructions on judging, however, never told us not to judge, only to realize that we would be judged by the same criteria (Matt. 7:1). Judging is, in fact, an essential element of living the Christian life. And judging is evaluating. Therefore, not only is judging a personal need, it is also a leadership responsibility. In fact, it is the only way church leaders can check their effectiveness.

What is worship?

Worship is a relationship with God. The English word worship is derived from the Anglo-Saxon *worthship* and carries the sense of bowing down in homage. Worshipping is attributing worth to an object. The Greek word carries the image of a dog crouching at its master's feet.[3]

God is the object of our worship and He has commanded us to worship Him, as Jesus instructed Satan, "You shall worship the Lord your God, and serve Him only" (Matt. 4:10). Believers are required to prostrate themselves before God in humble homage and complete submission. Worshipping is looking from ourselves to God, focusing on Him and presenting praise, adoration, love, submission—"worthship"—from the believer to God.

The current trend in the church toward the person in the pew passively observing and being entertained by platform professionals little resembles the concept of worship that is taught in the Scriptures. Such services have little potential for persons in the pew to be motivated to experience true worship of God, much less be enabled to perform outreach ministry through their lives. This is not to say that the only reason to worship is to produce outreach. The priority of worship services is still worship. The beneficial by-product of worship, however, is outreach ministry. Church leaders are accountable to God for the quality of worship their groups experience.

When believers truly experience worship, both church growth and increase in financial support usually follow. Worship, however, should not be contrived to achieve increase in growth and finances. True worship must be the goal whether it produces such results or not.

Scripture clearly identifies the rationale for worship. Many biblical references argue that worshipping God, not horizontal activity, is His highest priority for believers. God knows the benefits of worship, as observed in the words of the psalmist "In Thy presence is fulness of joy" (Ps. 16:11) and "for those who honor Me I will honor" (1 Sam. 2:30), are the very means for developing true believers. It is through this developed believer that God can then accomplish horizontal ministry to fellow believers and community.

What is outreach?

Believers have three relationships that are to be developed and maintained. These are to seek and build relationships first with God, then to other believers, and finally, to the community around them. A Scripture passage that points this out clearly is Acts 1:8. Jesus instructed believers to "...be My witnesses both in Jerusalem, and in all Judea and Samaria, and even to the remotest part of the earth." Thus, from the vertical relationship, we move to a horizontal interaction with other believers and then to reaching out to the communities around them.

Outreach takes many forms. It can be visitation, small group study, tract distribution, caring for the disadvantaged, and a host of other activities. The key is the motive for reaching out, not the act itself. Outreach that honors God gives Him glory, praise, adoration, and worship. In society's frantic pace, the church is caught up in programs and activities where success is the goal, rather than the worship and praise of God. Such programs and activities deter rather than encourage a relationship with God. Like Moses of old, church leaders are accountable to God for creating a worship setting that results in reaching out.

How can worship be evaluated?

For worship, church leaders should consider the following seven questions in their evaluation.[4]

Is there a specific written objective for the worship experience?
The first step in planning a worship experience is to establish a clear goal. This goal should be written in a statement that describes what the participants will be doing and experiencing as a result of worship. For example, "After of our Sunday

morning worship service on _____ (date) the congregation will demonstrate _____ (personal actions) as evidenced by _____ (measurable features)."

That may appear to be too structured, but it really isn't. It becomes the means by which the Holy Spirit can use each facet of the experience to produce the intended goals.

Does the setting encourage worshippers to focus on God?

Building design, seating arrangements, and all the physical features of the worship setting should encourage worshippers to focus on God. Studies show that buildings with low ceilings and crowded seating seriously detract from establishing a true worship experience. Though the setting does not have to be grand, its design and appearance should encourage dignity and respect. This also includes cleanliness, maintenance, and types of materials used.

Does the worship experience follow a planned progression?

People entering a worship setting come from a bewildering array of background problems and issues. In order to center on God, they need a planned transition from problems and issues to one in which God increasingly becomes the focus. From the beginning to the conclusion of the worship experience, individual concentration on God should build. Thus, every component of the experience—prayer, music, preaching, offering, Lord's Table, baptism, testimonials—should be designed to escalate concentration upon God.

Does the selected Scripture and the preaching magnify God?

People who are buffeted by the stresses and disappointments of life need to have those experiences seen in the reflection of whom God is. These life experiences need to also be seen in relationship to what He has done, what He is doing, as well as what He will do. This is not to minimize the problem of sin. The purpose of a worship experience is not to magnify sin but to magnify God. Neither is the purpose of the worship experience to magnify the speaker or teacher. The speaker or teacher is simply the instrument God uses to deliver His Word.

Does the music foster worshipping and praising God?

Unfortunately, much current Christian music only magnifies our relationships with each other, makes our requests of God, or simply entertains. Though each of these outcomes have their place in the church, they do not produce worship of God. Music must be carefully selected for both its musical composition and its message. This insures that the spotlight of attention in this entire experience is upon God and His attributes. Any music that has the performer or the music leader as the center of attention should have no place in any worship service.

The quality of the music must also be consistent with community standards. Music performances other than what is common for the participants in their community (city, theatre, local public groups, schools, etc.) will seriously detract from the worship experience desired.

Are the participants actively and positively involved?

In what creative ways are participants actually involved in the worship experience? Worship does not occur passively. There must be opportunities for participants to express their personal praise to God. How can participants express worship in giving their tithes and offerings? Where can the participant join in the singing, the prayer, the reading of the Scripture? Are the group experiences designed to produce personal involvement?

What evidences are there that true worship is occurring?

What are the indicators you, as church leaders, are willing to accept? Is there increased adoration of God, growth in personal development, spiritual maturity, individual life changes, congregational growth, financial increases? This is where leaders must go back to specific written objectives to determine whether they have achieved the goal or they now need to adjust activities to accomplish the intended results?

How can outreach be evaluated?

Following are seven questions church leaders should use to evaluate the church's outreach ministry.

Is the outreach ministry consistent with the church's written goals?

The goal should always be to do a few activities well rather than many activities mediocre. Has the church evaluated where its strengths and gifts are and employed these to its greatest effectiveness?

Is there adequate equipping and training offered to produce an effective outreach program?

Each church should have an ongoing resource pool of workers who have explored their ministry gifts and abilities and have completed basic training in a non-risk setting. In addition, the church should provide ongoing training options to sharpen the outreach ministry workers' skills.

What percentage of church attenders are serving in outreach ministries and what tangible results can be identified?

The most vibrant churches report that over 80% of attenders are active in various outreach ministries and that verifiable results can be identified with each ministry. If such results are not verified, that effort is terminated.

Is there sufficient ministry breadth to accommodate the wide interests and gifts of people?

Not every one will be drawn to Sunday School or choir. Are there creative and unique ministry opportunities for everyone?

Does outreach ministry reflect the concept that people win people?

Programs are not the most effective means to reach people; people are. Yet, programs are often accentuated over people. In the outreach ministry, how often and how meaningful is the contact between church workers and the community?

Are people from all backgrounds being reached?

Are ministry efforts properly spread over men and women, singles and married, children, youth, and adults?

Are outreach ministry leaders both relational and functional?

Since people win people, leaders must model positive inter-relational skills to those in the outreach ministry. These leaders also need those necessary skills to make the ministry effective and efficient.

Who does this evaluation?

Evaluation should be a function of a group rather than the professional church leaders. Evaluation is not a leadership function. Leadership uses the input from such evaluation as a means to determine what correctives may be needed to effectively accomplish the church's goals. When evaluation is carried out by the entire church membership, the members will exhibit much higher ownership and involvement and the results will be more accurate.

Two separate committees should be formed—one for worship and the other for outreach. These two committees should adopt criteria such as suggested above and seek congregational feedback with the use of devices such as pew cards and focus group discussions. Depending upon the church organizational structure, these committees must have high credibility and accountability in the church's decision-making process. This is also necessary to make the changes to create healthy worship experiences which produce positive outreach ministry.

Summary

Evaluation and leadership are facets of the same role. Effective leadership, however, also requires effective evaluation. Effective evaluation is not possible without the responsibility, authority, and accountability of the leader. Hence, leadership and evaluation are inseparable.

Some church leaders argue that their job descriptions do not obligate them to evaluate worship or outreach. That could be true. Since worship is so integral to the overall church ministry, however, all leaders must take some role in assuring that true worship occurs. Worship is not limited to what may take place on Sunday morning. Worship must also occur in all church members' lives wherever they may be. Worship affects all church leaders simply because worship affects all attenders.

Though the leader's duties may not require direct supervision over worship or outreach, it is in each leader's capability to influence the direction of the church in such matters. As soon as leaders accept their roles in a church, they also accept the reality that one day God will expect an accounting of that influence over others, even in the broadest of senses (James 3:1). Therefore, church leaders can secure a preview of that day of accountability by evaluating how well they have affected worship and outreach in the church.

Notes

1. George Barna, *What Americans Believe*, p. 61ff, Ventura: Regal Books, 1991.
2. Kennon L. Callahan, *Twelve Keys to an Effective Church*, p. 24ff, San Francisco: Harper and Row, 1983.
3. Robert L. Saucy, *The Church in God's Program*, p. 166ff.
4. Richard Patterson, "Evaluating Worship and Outreach," *Evaluating Your Church* (Ministering with Confidence series), Wheaton: Evangelical Training Association, 1991.

For further consideration

1. Study the word *worship* in a concordance to notice its uses in both the Old and New Testaments.
2. Analyze the importance the Bible gives to the use of worship in both the Old and New Testament in contrast to current church programs.

Application activities

1. Review the worship experiences of your church, both corporate and personal. Evaluate whether these experiences meet the criteria cited.
2. Write a plan of action for improving worship in your church that identifies your role and how this role will interact with other leaders in improving the quality of worship.
3. Do a similar review of the outreach experiences in your church. Write a plan of action to improve outreach effectiveness. Be sure the plan includes a part you can play.

7 NURTURE AND EQUIPPING AS MEASURES OF LEADERSHIP

All church leaders have the biblical responsibility for nurturing and equipping church members to minister in their world. Parachurch organizations might help the church in this dual goal of nurturing and equipping, but it is the primary responsibility of the church working through its leadership.

Measuring a leader's effectiveness is an important leadership function. Jesus taught this principle many times in the New Testament. Several of His parables stressed this truth (i.e. Luke 12:47,48; Matt. 21:33-36; 25:14-30). Using the nurture and equipping of others as measuring tools of one's leadership ability was also a Pauline principle. Paul told Timothy that how well he developed others was a strong indication of how effective he was as a leader. Paul carefully explained that he must use great care in selecting, nurturing, and equipping each person he placed into church ministry (1 Tim. 5:21,22). Finally, Paul tells Timothy that his future evaluation by God depends upon how effective he was in developing others (2 Tim. 4:8).

How nurture and equipping are related

Frequently, church programs stress either nurture (sometimes termed discipleship) or equipping (sometimes termed training) as though they were separate goals. In determining church worker goals, leadership development texts rarely relate nurture and equipping. Yet, the Bible often treats them together. Paul instructed Timothy that all Scripture was inspired by God and "profitable for teaching, for reproof, for correction, for training in righteousness; that the man of God may be adequate (nurtured to maturity), equipped (ready to serve Christ) for every good work" (2 Tim. 3:16,17). God's Word stresses that both nurture and equipping should be treated together as a dual goal in believers' lives.

52

Unfortunately, the trend in many churches is toward only discipling others, which stresses the development of the inner man. This discipling approach neglects helping the person to discover and employ their spiritual gifts to serve Christ in their world. Yet the Scriptures continually link the two saying that nurture should result in equipping believers to serve.

Though many biblical passages show this linkage, one of the more graphic is found in 1 Thessalonians 2:7. Here Paul used the nurture words of caring and gentleness and then follows these words with an equipping term of a trained and prepared nurse, and concluded by describing a caring ministry for others. Since the Bible links nurture and equipping, it is also necessary to associate the two when considering an evaluation strategy for church leaders.

What is the biblical pattern?

Searching the Scriptures reveals a clear pattern about the goals of nurture and equipping. The *source* of both nurture and equipping is always found in the Word of God (2 Tim. 3:16,17). First, though the church may use other resources to produce these goals, for determining truth such resources must always be considered inferior to the Scriptures. To insure truth, the Bible must serve as the grid through which all other resources flow. Second, God has gifted the church with leaders who should serve as the *means* for achieving this nurture and equipping (Eph. 4:11,12). Third, the *target* of nurture and equipping, as revealed in Ephesians 4:12-16, is: true maturity, unity of the faith, building of the Body of Christ, and service to one's community and the world. Thus, a definite scriptural pattern emerges for accomplishing nurture and equipping and must figure prominently in the leader's evaluation of both goals.

Defining nurture and equipping

Since there is a progression in these two goals, it is best to begin by defining both from the Scriptures. Nurture is that aspect of church ministry which focuses upon developing individual believers to discover, claim, and be all that their Creator designed His people to be.

Notice the progression in the definition of equipping. Equipping is that aspect of church ministry which focuses upon developing believers to minister efficiently and effectively in their world. The first definition emphasizes the person while the second centers more on what that person does. Both nurture and equipping are needed in the total development of all believers. Nurture must occur, so equipping can properly be done.

The Bible mentions four principles concerning nurture and equipping. They are:
- Both are Christ's plan for every believer—"Now the God of peace, who brought up from the dead the great Shepherd of

the sheep through the blood of the eternal covenant, even Jesus our Lord, equip you in every good thing to do His will, working in us that which is pleasing in His sight, through Jesus Christ, to whom be the glory forever and ever. Amen" (Heb. 13:20,21).

* Both require personal commitment—"Therefore, if a man cleanses himself from these things, he will be a vessel for honor, sanctified, useful to the Master, prepared for every good work" (2 Tim. 2:21).

* Both demand pursuing spiritual characteristics—"But flee from these things, you man of God; and pursue righteousness, godliness, faith, love, perseverance and gentleness" (1 Tim. 6:11).

* Both carry a need for struggle and suffering—"And after you have suffered for a little while, the God of all grace, who called you to His eternal glory in Christ, will Himself perfect, confirm, strengthen and establish you" (1 Pet. 5:10).

In addition, there are also four principles concerning when nurture and equipping should occur in the church. They are:

* When Christians believe they are called by God—"Who has saved us and called us with a holy calling, not according to our works, but according to His own purpose and grace which was granted to us in Christ Jesus from all eternity" (2 Tim. 1:9).

* When believers realize they have been sovereignly gifted—"But to each one is given the manifestation of the Spirit for the common good" (1 Cor. 12:7).

* When believers appreciate they will be evaluated by God for life ministry—"Each man's work will become evident; for the day will show it, because it is to be revealed with fire; and the fire itself will test the quality of each man's work" (1 Cor. 3:13). See also Matthew 25:14-30.

* When church leaders awaken to their true task—"And He gave some as apostles, and some as prophets, and some as evangelists, and some as pastors and teachers, for the equipping of the saints for the work of service, to the building up of the body of Christ" (Eph. 4:11,12).

How nurture and equipping differ from training

In my chapter in *Christian Education: Foundations For The Future*, I point out that the church and its leadership have serious problems staffing their ministries today because, for many years, they have stressed only training rather than nurturing and equipping their workers.[1]

To clear up any confusion between how the concept of nurture and equipping differs from training, consider the following:

* Nurture and equipping concentrates on the person, whereas training concentrates on the task.

- Nurture and equipping develop individual potentials, whereas training develops proficiency.
- Nurture and equipping teaches problem solving, whereas training teaches technique.
- Nurture and equipping begins new ministry, whereas training generally maintains existing ministry.
- Nurture and equipping focuses upon the goal, whereas training upon the process.

These distinctions are not intended to discredit training at the expense nurture and equipping, or vice versa. But it is done to show that the goal of nurture and equipping is developing believers for life ministry while training's goal is fulfilling a task. Since the church is a ministry and not a business, its goal should be developing people, not just fulfilling tasks.[2]

Evaluating nurture and equipping

Though this whole chapter is designed to help leaders evaluate the effectiveness of nurture and equipping ministries, the following questions should help in your general assessment.[3]

1. What evidences are there that all the believers you lead have a sense of calling from God in their lives?
2. Can you identify an individual nurture ministry that is distinct and separate from the preaching ministry?
3. Of all those you lead, are at least 60% participating in your nurture ministry?
4. If your nurture ministry is carried out entirely through the church educational ministry, how can you tell if both nurture and educational goals are being met?
5. Are equipping efforts directed to all believers in the church or just prospective leaders and workers?
6. Are your equipping and nurture efforts directly linked?
7. Have over 60% of those you lead completed your basic equipping program?
8. Does the equipping program you've created for your workers include the following components:
   a. discovery of self, gifts, call, and life design.
   b. comprehension of Bible survey and doctrinal beliefs.
   c. understanding of human development from a biblical perspective.
   d. ministry skills development.
   e. helping believers apply their ministry gifts and skills in non-threatening, low-risk church laboratory settings.
   f. evaluating ministry effectiveness with consequent commitment to lifelong learning.
9. Do both the nurture and equipping efforts of your leadership reflect the following motivators:

    a. opportunities are programmed to the workers' personal time schedules.

    b. workers see such efforts as meaningful.

    c. these efforts help workers build confidence.

    d. workers perceive true personal recognition.

    e. such experiences encourage a sense of personal achievement.

10. Have at least 60% of the participants initiated personal ministry to their community and world?

Although there is no set score to this set of questions, as you answer them, remember they reflect what many church consultants believe are the marks of effective church leaders.

Who should evaluate?

Each church has its own polity and organizational structure for determining how evaluations are conducted. Surely these factors should be considered in determining who should do the evaluating. However, if the total evaluation is left to the elected or appointed church officers, two results often occur. The church officers, or leaders, only see what they perceive to be true about such nurture and equipping, and lay people fail to build ownership of the leaders' nurture and equipping efforts.

Though it is essential that church leaders use the results of the evaluation of the nurture and equipping efforts under their leadership, leaders must seek more independent information than their own perceptions. Therefore, the recipients of the leaders' nurture and equipping efforts should be involved in the evaluation process. Such evaluations can be conducted in several ways.

A common way is to periodically take a simple survey of the workers under the leader's care. Questions which survey workers' feelings about how the nurture and equipping efforts are being carried out are better than questions which require objective responses. Leaders should want to know how their workers feel about their personal progress in those efforts.

Another approach might be to have leaders appoint a team to conduct one-on-one interviews. Much of this can be informal once an effective nurture and equipping program is operating. As the evaluation is conducted, however, a mechanism must be developed which will help make the necessary corrections. This mechanism should establish some degree of authority or influence whereby the team is responsible to a leader who is authorized to make the needed changes.

Remember, in evaluation, it is not what leaders do that is important, it is what happens in the lives of those they lead. All biblical evaluation principles stress that the function of leadership is to produce spiritual results in those they lead. Thus, effective leaders for Christ must devise evaluations which determine their effectiveness in producing sound worship, biblical outreach, and personal nurture and equipping. This type evaluation may be challenging to leaders' egos. It may place the leaders' self-esteem at risk. But it also is the only way in which church leaders can determine whether they are efficient (doing things right) or effective (doing right things), or both.

So much of the church's current health, its individual and corporate family, and how it penetrates the world with the message of the grace of God depends upon effectively nurturing and equipping its membership. Evaluating this area of church ministry is critical to the church's survival and success not only today, but in the future. Church leaders need to begin to take these evaluative steps now. Evangelical Training Association, as always, stands ready to help you make your nurture and equipping ministries the success you desire them to be.

This chapter is not intended to be an evaluative tool for your church's education program. A separate module for evaluating that ministry is available in the *Ministering with Confidence* audio cassette series titled *Evaluating Church Education.* That module deals with what the church education program should look like, what it should produce, and how to make it work to meet your church's goals. Throughout, it uses evaluative criteria to help leaders make their ministries successful.

Summary

Objectively measuring the leader's influence in the church is difficult.[4] As a result, many choose not to evaluate. They assume that when and where weakness occurs, it will soon surface and they will wait to deal with the issue then. However, that is reactive leadership.[5] It waits for the fire to build before taking steps to extinguish it. Conversely, proactive leadership, as presented in the Bible, takes the initiative to assess efficiency and effectiveness. Even though such assessment carries personal risk to ego and self-esteem, leaders realize evaluation is the only means they have to check their performance and to make whatever correctives are necessary to please God. Such correctives also are beneficial to the ultimate evaluation God has for leaders.

Regardless of their role, church leaders are responsible for nurturing and equipping every person they lead to be effective in serving Christ.[6] It is, therefore, prudent for leaders to develop personal ways to evaluate their performance in nurture and equipping.[7]

Notes

1. Robert Clark, Lin Johnson, Allyn Sloat, *Christian Education: Foundations for the Future,* Richard Patterson, "Equipping The Educational Staff," p. 481ff, Chicago: Moody Press, 1991.

2. David S. Luecke and Samuel Southard, *Pastoral Administration*, Irving, TX: Word, 1985.
3. Richard Patterson, *Evaluating Your Church*, Ministering With Confidence.
4. Richard Patterson, *Being A Christian Leader*, p. 37ff, Moody Correspondence School, 1985.
5. Jay A. Conger, *The Charismatic Leader*, p. 107ff, San Francisco: Jossey-Bass, 1989.
6. Myron Rush, *The New Leader*, p. 131ff, Wheaton: Victor Books, 1987.
7. Melvin J. Steinbron, *Can The Pastor Do it Alone?*, p. 143ff, Ventura: Regal Books, 1987.

For further consideration

1. Study the relationships of the words nurture, equipping, and perfection in your concordance.
2. Create personal definitions of discipleship, training, nurture, and equipping.

Application activities

1. Develop a continuing nurture and equipping experience, involving everyone you lead, that meets the criteria cited in this chapter.
2. Develop an evaluation strategy which will provide you, as leader, with objective information about the effectiveness of your nurture and equipping program for your workers. In this evaluation mechanism be sure to establish a strategy for making corrections in those areas that need attention.

THE ROLE OF LEADERSHIP IN FELLOWSHIP AND FINANCES

8

"I'm not responsible for the fellowship programs and finances; that's the board's responsibility." This was one Sunday school superintendent's reply when asked about his part in these important aspects of church ministry. Many church leaders react this way regarding their responsibility in the areas of fellowship and finances. Managers of other church ministries echo the same sentiment. Traditionally, overseeing fellowship and finances is left to someone else. In fact, often financial oversight is left to the elected or appointed treasurer and everyone assumes that fellowship just happens.

Typical church leaders, at all levels, spend little time in either fellowship or financial supervision. In the financial area, supervision usually is reactive, that is, disbursement needs are met as revenue accrues. In this chapter, however, neither fellowship nor finances are treated as peripheral areas for church leaders, regardless of their roles or titles. These two areas of church life have been demonstrated as dynamic elements of total congregational life, and thus, must impact all church leaders. Granted, some leaders do have direct responsibilities in these areas. The biblical principles presented in Ephesians 4:11-16, however, argue that whatever affects corporate church life is every church leader's responsibility.

Why treat these two functions together?

Since most literature on church leadership treat fellowship and finances separately, it seems strange to unite them here. Financial matters usually are considered administrative functions, while fellowship is most often left to the individual program leaders in the church. What value is there for church leaders to consider them together?

Many of today's experts in church administration feel they should be considered together.[1] They agree that finances and fellowship are directly related. That is, as the level of genuine fellowship increases in a church, so does financial giving. Notice they don't base their argument on a larger membership producing increased giving. On the contrary, the figures show that the opposite is true which troubles some of today's larger churches. The church experts report that as meaningful personal fellowship increases, so does personal giving. These highly documented studies show that the participation level correlates directly with the depth of fellowship in the congregation.[2]

Biblical model for fellowship and finances

Paul relates the concepts of fellowship with that of finances in several of his writings. In 2 Corinthians 8:1-6, Paul links the two in verse 4, "Praying us with much entreaty that we would receive the gift, and take upon us the fellowship of the ministering to the saints" (KJV). The thrust of Paul's argument is that the Macedonians saw themselves in such fellowship (as "brothers") to the saints, that this relationship prompted them to give sacrificially. Though they were geographically separated, the Macedonians were so involved with the saints in other parts of the world that they did not give out of a sense of guilt, nor of duty, but because their fellowship group was in need.

Defining fellowship and finances

To better see how fellowship and finances relate, you need to understand what both terms mean as they are used in this text.

Fellowship

As the word fellowship is used here, it refers to the biblical concept of *koinonia* which bears little resemblance to the coffee and doughnut variety of fellowship found in many of today's churches. On the contrary, *koinonia* is uniquely linked to, produced, and fostered by the Holy Spirit. Thus, fellowship may be defined as a relationship in the church which is personally and interpersonally meaningful. Fellowship groups are further described as warm, accepting, supportive, and nurturing small communities where life faith exploration occurs.

To determine the quality of fellowship in your church, construct a diagram of circles which can be used to compare segments of the membership. Draw one circle which represents the number of people involved (attend services or meetings regularly) in your church. Then, draw a second circle which comparatively represents the total church membership. Finally, draw a third circle representing the number of persons who are in fellowship groups as described above. Church consultants say that, in today's healthiest churches, the fellowship circle actually is the same or larger than the membership or involvement circles.[3] Completing these diagrams for your church will be very revealing regarding its current effectiveness and may also accurately predict its future health.

In the studies used by the experts in church administration, many of the surveyed churches had fellowship circles that were considerably smaller than either the membership or involvement circles. As will be shown later in this chapter, these conditions indicate an uncertain future for those churches.

Since people are basically searching for four elements in life, knowing them and their impact upon relationships in church life is essential to church effectiveness. The four elements people seek are: 1) personal value, 2) community belonging, 3) meaningful value patterns, and 4) future security.[4] Notice that people are not seeking high activity programs and time commitments, but are looking for others who are also searching for these four life elements and with whom they can explore a life of faith together.

Thus, fellowship activities which help people find these four elements in life will immediately and continuously attract them. Consequently, church leaders who desire to be more effective should structure fellowship groups so that all those they lead will realize these four elements. It is the leader's responsibility to see that these groups are warm, accepting, supportive, nurturing, and help members explore life faith together in low-risk settings.

Finances

For finances, the definition that is used here is the function of the church which includes both gifts to the church and its expenditures. To analyze the financial picture of a church, leaders need to determine the average amount people give who attend the worship services (total gift income divided by the number of people attending). In addition, leaders need to determine the total gift income from the church members (total gift income divided by the number of church members). These two numbers, when graphed over time, will usually show that gift income goes up in direct relation to increased fellowship, not church membership. Thus, meaningful fellowship produces increased gift income.

The relationship between fellowship and finances, however, is also on the expenditure side as well. That is, money always follows mission. The more people see themselves as true participants in the group and clearly understand the church's mission (rather than maintenance) as the goal of the group, increased giving results. People always give to people first, because they see people as integral to their fellowship. Second, people give to causes. And, finally, people give to programs. What do these priorities in giving say to church leaders? When fellowship experiences are meaningful to church members, they are highly motivated to give. There is a definite relationship between true fellowship and finances, both gifts and expenditures.

Going back to the first argument for a moment, once a church has determined its financial formula (gift income of those meaningfully participating in fellowship groups vs. gift income of members), it should compare these figures to similar churches, either in its denomination or other nearby churches. This analysis should help church leaders see how effective their fellowship program is.

Second, the church needs to recognize that each member functions in three separate neighborhoods. There is a relational, sociological, and geographical neighborhood for every person. In every case, however, the largest gifts always come from the relational neighborhood. Where individuals meaningfully relate to others, they are more highly motivated to give generously. Meaningful fellowship, thus, becomes the imperative for the proper funding of the church. Meaningful fellowship also is a strong measure of church leaders' effectiveness.

Evaluative criteria

Church leaders should use the following questions to assess their performance in the areas of fellowship and finances.

1. Is the fellowship circle (representing the numbers of persons truly participating) as least as large as the membership circle or involvement circle of those under your leadership?
2. How soon after the initial exposure to the church is the person drawn into one of these fellowship groups?
3. Do participants in these fellowship groups express that they experience warmth, acceptance, support, personal nurture, community, and low-risk life exploration?
4. Are there plans for future relationship groups to accommodate new people?
5. What is the date which marks the halfway point in the tenure of present church members (½ joined before that date, ½ joined after)? If more than 7-10 years, it reveals a poor fellowship program and strong potential for decline.
6. How does the per capita gift income compare to churches similar to yours?
7. If you are not in a building program, are total church expenditures about $400-$600 per person (small church), $700-$1500 (mid-sized), or $1,000-$1500 (large)?
8. Do you spend 50-60% of your church income on staff (small church), 35-50% (mid-sized), 25-45% (large)?
9. Do you spend 8-15% on missions (small church), 15-20% (mid-sized), 20-35% (large)?
10. Do educational expenditures carry the same priority as missions, physical plant, and salaries and represent 11-15% of the budget?

Who conducts this evaluation?

Committees already charged with other responsibilities should not have evaluation added to their duties. Rather, a new team of qualified and interested lay persons who are involved in both fellowship and finances should be appointed. This team can have a church officer participating with them. The evaluation team's format should insure that participants from both fellowship and finance groups can actively dialogue. Whatever way the evaluation group is constructed, it should have the authority to influence the church's decision-making process.

Bennis points out the differences between leading and managing. He says, "Many an institution is very well managed and very poorly led. It may excel in the ability to handle each day all the routine inputs yet may never ask whether the routine should be done at all." Often church leaders fall into this category, many are better managers than leaders. You may recall this distinction was made earlier. Good managers do things right, while good leaders do right things. Often church leaders do the wrong things well.

Church leaders often make a common mistake. Many do not want to take the responsibility for evaluating whether biblical fellowship is occurring, so they defer the decision to a higher body. Unfortunately, these higher church bodies usually have a full agenda as well, so serious evaluation of biblical fellowship never happens. Consequently, leaders do not have hard evidence of how effective they are as leaders, their groups suffer the typical organizational pains without the organism benefits, and diminished giving results. This is a very high price to pay for failing to evaluate your leadership in this important area.

Bennis further states two basic laws or principles of leadership. His first law states, "Routine work drives out nonroutine work and smothers to death all creative planning, all fundamental change...in the institution." His second is, "Make whatever grand plans you will, you will be sure the unexpected or the trivial will disturb and disrupt them." These two principles affect the church leader's ability to create and sustain the experiences that produce biblical fellowship. Effective church leaders need to marshall all their strength and abilities toward realizing these goals, or such goals will simply be unfulfilled dreams.

Lyle Schaller adds another important leadership principle. He says that each church needs to determine whether it seeks to be a community of believers or a community of communities. He describes a community of believers as the entire group of worshippers in a given church. While his description of a community of communities is, "To conceptualize that church as a congregation of many smaller caring, supportive, loving, and closely knit communities." It is interesting to note that Schaller sees these two consequences as options. As a leading church consultant, he says that the community of believers option causes the church to remain static in growth for the future while the community of communities produces strong future growth. This is not to say that one option is better than the other. It means that if growth is a goal, it must adopt the model of community of communities. There are advantages and disadvantages to both options. Thus, leaders' tasks can be further complicated by their churches' mission and goal statements.[5]

Summary

Though some church leaders believe their role in fellowship and finances is quite limited, the Bible teaches differently. Whatever helps the body of Christ grow spiritually is the church leader's responsibility.[6] Surely, some church leaders' job descriptions specifically target either fellowship or finances. Yet, since the quality of fellowship directly affects both giving and spending in the church, such responsibility cannot be limited to just those job descriptions. Nurturing biblical fellowship which produces the biblical goals of Christ's church is an imperative element of every church leadership role.

Since biblical fellowship occurs most readily in small groups, creating and encouraging such groups should be every church leader's task. Understanding how fellowship influences finances validates the role of church leaders in those elements of the church program.

Leading congregations differs from managing them. By working with the details of existing programs, managers seek to make them efficient and cost-effective. Managers also tend to maintain the status quo. If the church desires to develop biblical fellowship, however, it requires the skills of an effective leader rather than a manager.

Every lamb wants and needs a shepherd. Sheep long for their shepherd's direction, guidance, protection, and loving care. In order to cultivate the biblical concept of fellowship, church leader/shepherds must direct, guide, protect, and lovingly care for their sheep.

Notes

1. Warren Bennis, *Why Leaders Can't Lead*, p. 14-16, San Francisco: Jossey-Bass, 1989.
2. Kennon L. Callahan, *Twelve Keys to an Effective Church*, p. 104ff.
3. Lyle Schaller and Charles Tidwell, *Creative Church Administration*, p. 192ff, Nashville: Abingdon Press, 1975.
4. Kennon L. Callahan, *Twelve Keys to an Effective Church*, p. 104ff.
5. Lyle E. Schaller, *Choices for Churches*, p. 63ff, Nashville: Abingdon Press, 1990.

6. Lloyd Perry, *Getting The Church On Target*, p. 144ff, Chicago: Moody Press, 1977.

For further consideration

1. Secure a Bible concordance which has Greek words cited along with the English usage and look up the references for *koinonia*, biblical fellowship.
2. From this study, develop several principles about biblical fellowship.
3. Study the Bible passages cited in the chapter for the relationships between fellowship and finances. What additional insights do you see?

Application activities

1. Employ the criteria questions cited in this chapter for those areas in the church that you lead. Do the fellowship circle activity as described and establish a diagram of existing conditions.
2. Envision and write a plan of action that will take your sheep into greener pastures concerning biblical fellowship in your church. Cite not only the goals, but each step necessary to reach those goals.

9 THE REALITY OF POWER AND LEADERSHIP

Power—the very word seems to suggest evil. Powerful dictators, powerful mafia, powerful drug lords; the list seems endless. However, power can be described otherwise. For believers, and especially for church leaders, power should be interpreted in a much broader context.

Defining power

The dictionary defines power in various ways, some of which are rather complicated. It says that power is strength and vigor, the ability to act, the authority to do, the control of a government, the magnifying capacity of a lens, and, in mathematics, the number of times as indicated by an exponent that a number occurs as a factor in a product.

For our purposes realize that power is a natural entity; it can be either good or evil. It is good when properly used, but evil when abused. Power is good when used to accomplish God's design, but can be evil when used for our own gain.

According to Habecker, leadership cannot be studied without discussing power, for power is the capability of doing or affecting something. Power, he says, "underlies the entire spectrum of ways to influence behavior."[1] Power is a gift God created and has extensive potential for both good or evil. It is capable of causing change. Power is the ability to influence decisions and planning for good or evil. Power is a mighty force in the church, especially during times of aggressive change and stress.

According to Campolo, power is the basic drive of every human being. Thus, he says, people play power games on a continuing basis.[2] Granted, this hunger for power is stronger in some persons than others and is varied in its expressions. Some people seek power over circumstances and others over their environment. Some people wield power over other's behavior, feelings, and thinking. Sadly, many believers fall into one or more of these groups.

The uses of power

Power can be legitimate or illegitimate. When leaders use power to fulfill God's plan or will, they use power legitimately. Be careful, though, not to rationalize an abuse of power, interpreting it as God's will, or as a license to dictatorially get our own way. You may recall in Genesis 2:19 God brought all the animal world to Adam, asking him to give each a name. This was legitimate power. Even though this event occurred before the fall, don't assume that the use of power is the result of sin. It is not—the abuse of power resulted from the fall.

Power is employed illegitimately when it is used to fulfill selfish goals. This rationale certainly is in vogue today just as it was in Bible times. A biblical example is found in Philippians 4. Two women, Euodia and Syntyche, co-workers with Paul, were playing power games with each other. It was affecting the entire Philippian church. They had taken opposing positions and gathered their own followers. Using religion as a mask, they were abusing power to achieve their own selfish goals. This power play seriously threatened the unity of that church. As a response, Paul wrote the letter to the Philippians.

According to humanistic rationale, people need to use power illegitimately in order to accomplish their goals in life. This is true in the church, the community, or the family. In human rationalization (humanism), people believe power gives them personal value or self-esteem. Therefore, it should not surprise us when illegitimate uses of power surface in the church. It is simply what the world has taught us to do to achieve value.

The drive for power is basic to humanity and the world teaches through its value system that it is acceptable to use power, whether legitimately or illegitimately. In God's eyes, however, this is not true. Schaller warns church leaders that although power can be distributed to each person in the group, such power can also, "Still the prophetic voice, thwart proposals for change, and perpetuate the status quo."[3] Thus, inhibiting the power of the majority can be anti-democratic while squelching the power of the minority (leadership) can prevent accomplishing goals. Finding the best solution to this problem often requires church leaders to acheive a delicate balance.

The source of power

Believers need to remember that all power belongs to God. He is the Creator and Sustainer. All power in this world is rooted in God. The psalmist said, "Some boast in chariots, and some in horses; but we will boast in the name of the Lord, our God" (Ps. 20:7). Thus, even when someone illegitimately uses power, God is the source of that power. Theologically, abusing something God created and that is a component of His nature, must not only offend God, but also bring His retribution. Although a somber thought, it is a biblical theme from Genesis to Revelation. Every time persons or groups used power to achieve personal goals, God responded in retribution.

Thus, not only it is irritating when someone abuses power in the church, it also always brings divine retribution either on the person or the group. Therefore, tolerating power abuse in the church has deadly repercussions. Any reading of Revelation chapters 2 and 3 will confirm this.

Authority and power

Authority and power are different. Authority is the formal aspect of power; while power can be exercised very effectively without one having authority. Some of the strongest power influences in your leadership area may originate from persons who have no authority. Authority can also use power legitimately or illegitimately, at whatever level or position in the church.

The presence of power

An old adage found in management literature says, "Power never occurs in a vacuum." This simply means that power always happens in every setting. The power to influence, the power to change, the power to cause, is in every situation, be it church, community, workplace, or family. If church leaders choose not to exercise legitimate power in a given situation, someone else will, whether authorized or not. And the power that is exercised may well be illegitimate. Hence, church leaders need to remember that if they choose not to exercise legitimate power, someone will attempt to use illegitimate power. This principle is basic to resolving church conflicts.

Types of power

Church leaders will encounter ten types of power. Knowing these types will help them know where to expect power intervention and will also help them in understanding themselves.

Positional

Positional power is derived from the position one has with the group. It can be an elected or appointed office, such as pastor, chairperson, superintendent, or director. It can also be the status the group has chosen to give to that person.

Reputational

The abilities of a person outside the group, in matters unrelated to the group, can be reputational power. This can be significant power. The person, for example, who successfully holds a major administrative position in business, can wield a strong reputational power in an unrelated group.

Coalition

Coalition power is gained from separate sources who realize they have greater power when joined together. That is, rather than demonstrating their individual power against an objection, they find that by forging an alliance with other power sources (with whom they may not normally align), they can exercise enough power to overcome the objection blocking their goal.

Communicational

People who have better verbal or writing skills than others carry a unique power of their own. This is known as communicational power. The great orators and literary giants throughout history have all been able to exercise power upon their settings far beyond that of others. Church leaders can conclude that by sharpening their communication skills, they also increase their potential for power.

Success

In this type of power, the success one has had in other areas provides a power not necessarily related to the setting. For example, the person holding a Ph.D. degree in science is often seen as an expert in other areas such as sports, auto repair, etc.

Financial

The wealthy person, and the potential application of that wealth to the goals of the group, wields extensive power. Obviously this wealthy person can unduly influence the group toward goals that are personal.

Personality

Some personalities have such magnetic charm or irresistible impact, they intimidate others. They may deny such influence. Yet it is a very powerful force.

Program

This type of power is derived from programs that have been historically successful in helping the group achieve its goals. For example, when considering budgetary requirements, if a music program has had unusual success, it can exercise power far beyond that of the Sunday School or the youth ministry.

Dedication

Persons who show unusual dedication and loyalty to a task have created a power of recognizable value. If this person, who is so tireless and worked so hard for the organization, feels negative about an issue, this person can sway the group far beyond the facts of the issue.

Spiritual

Similar to dedication, but in a positive sense, people who are truly spiritual persons, who are deeply committed to the Word of God, whose prayer lives show genuine maturity, carry a strong influence among their colleagues.

Take time here to assess your own power type. Following is a self-test which will help you determine which power type you are and where you can expect confrontation from others. Answer each of these questions prayerfully and in some depth. They will be critical in helping you solve many of the conflicts you may experience as a church leader.

1. Of those listed, what types of power do I have?
2. What is the source of my power in my daily life?
3. What have been the consequences when I have used this power?
4. What would others say about my use of power?
5. What evidences can I cite where my use of power glorified God?
6. What evidence is there that, when I've recognized the power types in others, I've either used or accommodated them in my leadership?
7. In what circumstances can I expect to find power confrontations in my church leadership?

This exercise will help church leaders gain insight into who they are as leaders of power. It also serves to forewarn them of situations where they can expect power sources to emerge in conflict to them as leaders. It should also tell leaders whether they tend toward legitimate or illegitimate uses of power. It guides church leaders in assessing their effectiveness in the proper use of power.

The leader's use of power

Though this topic was introduced earlier in this chapter, it will be broadened and furthered illustrated here. Four features that should earmark the leader's use of power are: 1) Jesus is the model to follow, 2) leaders need to understand what power means to them, 3) leaders need to check their motives, and 4) leaders must be sure they are accountable for their power.

Jesus is the model to follow

Since it is not possible to be effective church leaders without using power, it is essential that they follow a proper model of power. Jesus, of course, is that model. Jesus was the most powerful person who ever lived. Yet, He used that power appropriately and focused it upon God-honoring goals. Church leaders need to consider two thoughts here.

First, in following Christ's model, they need to exercise power only after this power potential has been submitted to the lordship of Christ. It is entirely possible that leaders will assume that because they have God-honoring goals, their process of using power must also be God-honoring. The two, however, are not synonymous. Leaders need to question their motives as well as their methods for using power. The measurement question is

"Has the exercise of power in every circumstance been submitted to the lordship of Christ?"

Secondly, leaders must process this power toward goals that are God-honoring. Thus, motive, means, and end results are all part of the way leaders exercise their power. In every case, each element of power must be submissive to the model Jesus presented. Church leaders must not refrain from using power in their leadership roles but must recognize that power is the tool God intended them to use.

Understand what power means to you

Gardner helps church leaders understand what power should mean to them when he says, "Power is not to be confused with status or prestige. It is the capacity to ensure the outcomes one wishes and to prevent those one does not wish. Power...is simply the capacity to bring about certain intended consequences in the behavior of others."[4] Leaders must not shrink away from power any more than they should not use it for personal gain. Power is the means God intends for leaders to achieve goals that honor Him. Acts 1:8 reports that God sent His Spirit so that believers would have the necessary power to accomplish His purposes on this earth.

Check your motives

Since the use of power is so delicate, leaders must analyze their innermost motives each time they use power. The carnal nature can lure leaders into abusing power. Even their reasoning can be distorted when employing power. Each time leaders exercise power in their church leadership roles, it is a spiritual exercise. It is an action leaders will need to account for when they stand before the Lord.

Be sure you are accountable in your power

Power is one of most corrupting forces humans know. The principle is very true, "power tends to corrupt; absolute power corrupts absolutely." Habecker cites Richard Foster, as he says, "Those who are accountable to no one are especially susceptible to the corrupting influence of power... Today, most media preachers and itinerant evangelists suffer...from the same lack of accountability that the wandering prophets of the sixth century did."[5] One of the checks on the abuse of power is for leaders to be accountable to others in all uses of power. This is not to say that leaders must secure permission prior to using power. It means that every leader must know, without a doubt, that all exercises of power are subject to review, and are being monitored, by human authority beyond them. Allowing anyone to use power in any group without such accountability will always produce abuse of power.

Summary

To be a leader is to exercise power. Leadership isn't possible without power. How that leadership is manifested, however, is critical to church leaders. Jesus told His disciples they were not to exercise power as the gentiles (or unbelievers), but to exercise power as servants (Luke 22:25,26). Since all power belongs to God, church leaders exercise power as stewards in His stead. Such power applications carry heavy responsibilities to God.

Power can be either legitimate or illegitimate. Thus, it is important for church leaders to recognize both expressions. It is also necessary for church leaders to be able to discern the various power types. In so doing, they can anticipate illegitimate intervention and conflict, as well as develop leadership strategies to cope with such power uses. Leaders can harness the positive power types toward achieving proper group goals.

Notes

1. Eugene B. Habecker, *The Other Side of Leadership*, p. 33-34, Wheaton: Victor Books, 1987.
2. Anthony Campolo, Jr. *The Power Delusion*, p. 9, Wheaton: Victor Books, 1983.
3. Lyle E. Schaller, *The Change Agent*, p. 140, Nashville: Abingdon Press, 1972.
4. John W. Gardner, *Leadership and Power*, p. 3, Independent Sector, 1986.
5. Richard Foster, *Money, Sex, and Power*, p. 178-179.

For further consideration

1. Using a topical Bible study guide, conduct a study about the good and evil uses of power. Try to find principles in both good and evil uses of power that can serve you in how you use power?
2. Review the organizational chart for your church. What positions reflect the types of power cited in the chapter? What other types of power do you anticipate are also in your church?

Application activities

1. Imagine your church is embarking on a new era in the area of your leadership responsibility. As the leader in this area, what will your people expect from you concerning why, where, when, and what these new programs or endeavors will be?
2. What types of power will you find necessary to use to assure that this new venture will be successful?
3. What types of power do you expect will be detrimental to accomplishing these goals?
4. What strategy will you employ to assure goals are achieved?

LEADING DESPITE DIFFICULT PEOPLE

10

One of the most challenging tasks leaders face is working with difficult people. As society becomes increasingly stressed, conflicts surface. As a result, church leaders often become frustrated, encounters lead to despair and sometimes culminate in leaving their positions. Conflict seems to be inevitable in leadership. John Haggai calls this the time for "staying power."[1] Eims says this will take "tough love and leadership."[2] Engstrom and Larson write that leaders need "courage—swimming against the current."[3] Leading despite difficult people is as old as the Bible itself. In each case where leaders accomplished great things for God, difficult people often resisted. Time nor technology changes this inevitability. If you are a leader, you will sometimes need to work with difficult people.

Chapter 3 presented the basics for understanding people. In review, every person is created in God's image and He has carefully defined everyone's capabilities. Although sin has ruined God's image beyond human repair, correction is not beyond divine reach. Through redemption, by trusting Jesus Christ as Lord and Savior for salvation, people are "born again."

In this converted state, believers have a three-fold capability. First of all, they are able to know God's Revelation (Isa. 55:9; Rom. 1:19,20). Second, they have the capability to be perfect in a positional, progressive, and prophetic sense (Matt. 5:48). This perfection is the purpose of Scripture, the plan for the ministry, and the premise for teaching. And third, believers have been given special gifts by the Spirit of God. Although some disagree about the exact number of these gifts, many believe there are 19. They are usually grouped in three different categories: speaking gifts, serving gifts, and signifying gifts.

What may be hard for church leaders to appreciate is that each difficult person they deal with is also a recipient of this three-fold capability and the potential for correction is very

73

high. It is in this spirit leaders should approach each difficult person and conflict.

Remember also that each person has a temperament/personality generated both by genetics and environment. Each of these temperament/personality types have both strengths and weaknesses. Knowing the strengths and weaknesses for each type will help church leaders greatly in dealing with people. For further information on these temperament/personality types consult books such as *Transformed Temperaments*[4] and others.

Searching for self-worth

Such secular philosophers as Marx, Freud, and Frankl have tried to determine basic causes for behavior, but they did not consider what the Bible says about man. An exception, however, is the Christian psychologist, Larry Crabb. Crabb asserts that every person's basic drive is personal self-worth. He notes that before the Fall, people had two basic attributes—significance and security—which were met in a relationship with God.[5]

Significance and security in the Bible

Before the fall, God gave man a responsibility with major significance—naming the animals (Gen. 2:19). In addition, verse 25 speaks of major security when it says that Adam and Eve were so secure in their relationship with God that clothes were inconsequential. Though naked, they were not ashamed.

Significance is described as purpose, importance, and meaningfulness. Security can be defined as unconditional love which is permanently expressed. Both these basic needs were satisfied through a direct relationship with the Lord. Thus, these needs were attributes or characteristics of prefallen man.

After the Fall, however, a dramatic change occurred. Although they were attributes, significance and security now became unsatisfied needs due to their broken relationship with God. Both Adam, Eve, and their descendants now struggled with their environmental creation. They no longer had significance nor security (Gen. 3:10).

Each person's basic drive is for significance and security—the producers of self-worth. While both significance and security are the forces behind all behavior, the drive for significance is more prominent in men while security is more important to women.

Attaining self-worth through performance

The dilemma for church leaders is that today's society strongly declares that both significance and security are only satisfied through people's performances. That is, the better they perform, the greater the significance and security they can enjoy. Unfortunately, this premise is seriously flawed. How much performance is enough? What about times when performances fail? The sad truth is that millions in our society hunger for both significance and security but are chasing the wrong means for attaining them.

Sadly, this philosophy has also crept into the church. These two needs have been ecclesiastically distorted. The church frequently preaches and teaches that people's value lies in their performance, the amount they give, the time and energy with which they serve, and their faithfulness in attending church meetings. All are measures of performance. When people's performances do not measure up, the church often uses guilt to motivate them to make corrections. As a result, the church erodes people's self-worth. Performance never builds self-worth —only relationships can.

Establishing relationship-oriented behavior

Church leaders, therefore, must make correctives. They must make it clear to all in the church that their personal self-worth will only be satisfied and achieved in a proper relationship with God. Since self-worth, produced by significance and security, is the basic drive for every human, it is critical for leaders to properly understand and teach this concept to their people.

Thus, when leaders encounter people who are searching for significance through performance, such as seeking a church office, personal prominence, or special status, decisive action is crucial. They need to help the person turn from performance to relationship-oriented behavior. Most of the difficult people leaders conflict with are those who are seeking significance or security through performance.

At the root of all incorrect behavior is always erroneous thinking. Church leaders' responsibilities before God are to help those under their leadership to exercise right beliefs about what will make them feel significant and secure. Leaders will never be successful trying to change people only through exhortation and challenge. People modify their behavior only as they change their thinking. Interestingly, Jesus embraced this idea when He said, "But the things that proceed out of the mouth come from the heart, and those defile the man. For out of the heart come evil thoughts, murders, adulteries, fornications, thefts, false witness, slanders" (Matt. 14:18,19).

Unfortunately, the continuum does not stop with incorrect behavior, it carries on to produce erroneous feelings. Thus, as leaders are faced with difficult people and circumstances, they need to concentrate on changing these people's thinking for as they think, they act; as they act, they feel.

Again, begin with the basic premise of *relationship with God* producing positive self-worth as opposed to *performance for God*. At this point leaders might be thinking, "Isn't performance important, or even necessary?" Certainly, that is true. Performance is necessary, but it must be founded in a relationship with

God. The Bible makes this quite clear. It says that when people have a right relationship with God they can then achieve self-worth. Pharisaic legalism in the New Testament clearly illustrates the futility of reversing this principle. Yet society today continues to teach that satisfying the search for significance and security only comes through performance.

Church leaders must continue to change such distorted thinking. In doing so, they will eliminate most of the stress and injury related to dealing with difficult people.

Types of difficult people

Church leaders will encounter several types of difficult people. The seven patterns of behavior cited here are the most common in the church. In each case, however, the person displaying such difficult behavior is doing so as a result of a fruitless search for self-worth. Though it may sound overly simplistic, helping these persons to think correctly will begin to produce improved behavior and correct feelings about themselves and others. Though correcting their thinking is the basic strategy, to effectively work with such persons, leaders also need to use specific techniques. In each case, the type of behavior is described and followed by suggestions for working with that particular type.

Hostile type

Hostile persons have aggressive natures. They have temperaments and personalities which lead to this type of behavior. They often are either the first born in their family or an only child. Thus, their behavior may be genetically or environmentally caused. These persons also have learned behavioral techniques which have worked for them in the past—throwing tantrums, bullying others, intimidating the opposition, using injurious remarks. Of course, learned behaviors should be able to be unlearned. Although, changing a childhood behavior may be beyond church leaders' capabilities, this is where they must begin the process of changing this poor behavior.

Techniques for dealing with these people take three directions. First, leaders must confront such behavior without arguing. Argument is what hostile people seek. They think that winning the argument will produce victory, or significance, for them. Leaders must deny them this victory by not arguing. Nonetheless, they must confront these persons with an opposing viewpoint—either their own or the group's.

Second, leaders must control their own behavior. These people can produce rage in leaders' hearts and generate feelings of anger, hurt, and injury. Leaders must rise above their feelings and keep them in control. To lose control of your feelings gives victory to hostile people. It confirms to them they are using the right control tactic and thus gain significance for themselves.

Third, leaders must carefully listen to what hostile people say and take it seriously. Be sure that they are allowed to express their opinions or viewpoints and that they understand you realize how important their opinion or viewpoint is to them.

Keep in mind, though, it is either the drive for significance or security through performance that is fueling hostile people's behaviors. Placating them, yielding to them, compromising with them, may well feed their perception that such behavior is proper for them to achieve self-worth.

Indecisive type

The difficulty with indecisive people is that they postpone decisions. They have learned that if they ignore them long enough, the need for making decisions usually disappears. Indecisive people often are also perfectionists who believe they cannot decide until they have every possible fact. Since that is idealistic, decisions are rarely made. People in this category can be very difficult to work with on boards and committees, since they tend to influence others into non-action.

Behind their indecision is fear that they will lose security. They fear making an incorrect decision will cause the loss of some significance as well as security. Thus, the technique for working with this type has this truth basic to each step. Leaders need to take necessary steps to insure that these people are encouraged to freely express their viewpoint in a non-threatening setting.

Second, after carefully hearing their objection, leaders need to confront these persons with a minimum number of alternatives. This can be done by summarizing their viewpoints in your own words, asking whether this expression is accurate, and offering an alternative viewpoint. The alternative needs to be broken down into small pieces. Ask them for their response to each piece. By carefully working through their reactions to each piece of the alternative, you can usually help them find sufficient security to change their viewpoint.

✗ Complainer type

Somewhat similar to the previous type, complainers tend to incessantly gripe about almost everything, without making suggestions for how to correct anything. These people can always identify problems to solve, but rarely see issues to address. They prefer to just complain.

An effective technique for working with complainers is to just allow them to let off steam. Complainers must have a platform to air their views. No leader enjoys this process, yet, it is usually the only way for them to acknowledge complainers' feelings and assure they have had their day in court. Empathize, but don't sympathize, with complainers. That is, seek to understand, but not necessarily agree with them. Ask factual, problem-solving questions. Complainers usually have a factual issue, but they also have surrounded this fact with intense feelings. Solving the issue for them is to strip away the feelings from the facts.

Finally, ask complainers how they would like things to be resolved. Put them on the defensive in problem-solving. They believe they are most valuable when they point out errors. Help them discover that they are more valuable when point out errors and they work with the group toward solutions. Relating to the group toward solving problems, as opposed to the complainer's individualist mentality, is much more effective in producing healthy self-worth.

Negative type

This type people suffer from serious erosion of security. In their mind, every issue or suggestion has insurmountable obstacles. Negative types often respond with, "It won't work," or "We've tried that before." Often this spirit spreads through the group bogging down important issues. Christian groups seem to attract negatives types. Perhaps because believers desire everyone to agree on issues, they tend to overextend sympathy and cooperation to the negative types, regardless of the facts.

Leaders need to be optimistic, though realistic, with negative people. They need to feel their concerns are not only expressed, but also understood. Since these people are not necessarily looking for solutions, leaders should not offer them too quickly. Refrain from trying to convince negative types that things are not so bad. Instead, confront each facet of their issue, offering suggestions or contingency plans for solving the problem.

Uninvolved type

People falling in this category prefer to remain uncommitted. Rather than risk being rejected, criticized, or challenged, they choose to be silent. Until nearly everyone goes in a direction, until there is safety in joining a position, the uninvolved stay aloof. Although uninvolved types appear harmless on the surface, by remaining uncommitted, they are not working toward group solutions; hence, they are contributing to group problems.

Leaders should probe this type of person with open-ended questions; those that cannot be answered with a simple yes or no. Require the uninvolved to express an opinion. You may need to stare at them in a friendly manner for significant periods of time to prompt them to respond. Ask for meaningful responses to such questions as "What does it mean when...?" Leaders tend to eventually dismiss the uninvolved types. This type of person, however, though uncommittal in public, often is quite vocal when leaders are not present. Tactfully, gently, but firmly draw out their opinions. This public expression will reduce behind-the-scenes conflicting viewpoints.

Know-it-all type

Due to their misplaced desire to achieve significance through performance, know-it-all types have a tremendous need to demonstrate superiority. Their usual approach is to make the leader feel foolish, incompetent, or uninformed. They frequently are quite successful at this. Know-it-alls comprise two types of people. Some are genuine experts who are always reminding the leader and/or the group of their superiority. Others are phony experts who pompously seek attention to gain significance.

Since leaders need to use a different tactic with the each type, you need to first decide into which category each know-it-all falls—the genuine expert or the phony.

With a true expert, you need to do your homework before bringing up any issue. Don't try to talk "off the top of your head." Face the true expert with facts. Be specific, but not dogmatic. Place the expert in a defensive position by asking questions like "how would that make a difference to the issue under consideration?" As leader, be prepared to use what true experts have to offer, without yielding power.

The phony expert requires another approach. Though the leader must always respond with the facts to the jibes of the phony know-it-all, always provide opportunities for this person to save face. Give them a way out in a gracious manner. Overcome their objection with superior homework and knowledge of the facts, but allow them to keep a sense of dignity in defeat.

Super-supporter type

Super-supporters desperately need to be accepted by others. Thus, in an attempt to make people like them, they agree with whatever anyone suggests, whether they feel it is actually true or not. In the leader's presence, they are usually very supportive, agreeable, and sincere, often accepting tasks which they know will win the leader's favor. Frequently, however, super-supporters cannot follow through on their commitments. Conflict with the leader often results. In addition, super-supporters tend to be much less committed and agreeable when the leader is not present. In their constant quest for acceptance, they yield to the opinion of whoever they are talking with at the time.

Obviously, this type of person will be a serious problem unless identified and changed. This is the leader's role. Knowing these people need your favor, encourage them to express their true feelings and opinions, without any suggestion that a difference of opinion may reap your displeasure.

At the outset, recognize that these people may have difficulty following through and provide a way for them to get help in completing the task. Since super-supporters are so agreeable, often leaders forget that they need to constantly encourage these people to follow through.

Summary

Leaders live in an imperfect world which contains many difficult people. Even churches are often less than ideal environments. Yet, such has always been the case for God's leaders throughout history. Church leaders need to review what God says about people, their capabilities and gifts. In so doing, leaders must be convinced that, apart from Spirit of God working in every person's heart, dealing with difficult people would be nearly impossible. Thus, leaders need to wholeheartedly depend upon the Lord in fulfilling their leadership role.

Remembering that sin has driven people to seek significance and security, church leaders must constantly stress the foundational truth that these needs can only be met in a proper relationship with God. Then, in order to effectively relate to and work with the different types of difficult persons, leaders need to identify and treat each individual accordingly.

Notes

1. John Haggai, *Lead On*, p. 149ff, Irving, TX: Word, 1986.
2. Leroy Eims, *Disciples in Action*, p. 153ff, Wheaton: Victor Books, 1981.
3. Ted W. Engstrom and Robert C. Larson, *Seizing The Torch*, p. 115ff, Ventura, CA: Regal Books, 1988.
4. Tim LaHaye, *Transformed Temperaments*, Wheaton: Tyndale House, 1971.
5. Larry Crabb, *Understanding People*, Grand Rapids: Zondervan, 1987.

For further consideration

1. Do a Bible search to find biblical figures who reflect the types of difficult people cited in the chapter.
2. Study the creation account found in Genesis 1. What distinguishing features can you find in the creation of humans which are not found in the rest of creation?

Application activities

1. Place those persons under your leadership into the types of difficult persons cited in the chapter. Describe each one in detail.
2. Try to predict how the difficult people identified above will react and respond to ideas you might like to introduce in your church. What will you do to try to cope with them?

RESOLVING CONFLICT THROUGH LEADERSHIP $\overline{\underline{11}}$

The intent of this chapter is to help leaders see where conflicts often surface in the church and understand what they can do to creatively resolve them.

Why conflict?

Perhaps because stress is so prevalent in our society and the media keeps it on everyone's mind, church leaders are prone to think that the conflict they are continuing to encounter is new to today's world. The New Testament, however, is replete with illustrations of conflicts in the early church. Flynn lists several:
- the Greeks vs. the Hebrews (Acts 6:1-6)
- Paul vs. Peter, for his open prejudice (Gal. 2:11-14)
- Peter vs. the Judaizers (Acts 11:2,3)
- Paul vs. Barnabas (Acts 15:36-40)
- the Corinthian church vs. itself (1 Cor. 1:11,12; 6:1-11; 11:18-23)
- the Roman church vs. itself (Rom. 14:1-6)
- Euodia vs. Syntyche (Phil. 4:2,3)
- the Philippian church vs. itself (Phil. 2:14)
- the Jerusalem church vs. itself (James 4:1)
- Diotrephes vs. the church (3 John 9,10)[1]

Someone has said, "instead of majoring in communion, the church, through the ages, is muddled in contention." Others have said in jest, "To dwell above with saints we love; that will be glory. To dwell below with saints we know, well, that's a different story." It appears that conflict in the church is not new. This does not give conflict license, but it does give perspective. The cause is not the stress of our times, it is rooted in every person's struggle for power along with the variety with which God has created us.

Examining each of the conflicts recorded in the Bible reveals certain territories where such conflict emerges. They are:

- psychological—This represents conflict due to people's differing personalities and temperaments.
- sociological—This area has to do with the differing learning, behavioral, and decision styles that each person has.
- physical—Not only does this area encompass that conflict between male and female, but between age and racial groups as well.
- positional—This conflict territory has to do with one's position in the organization or group. For example, simply because one is in a role of authority, whether in the church or family, that position generates a potential for conflict.
- religious—Here we mean those differences of opinion, interpretation, or denominational upbringing and background that have been conflict areas for centuries.

Each of these areas are represented in the biblical conflict illustrations listed above. Since such background information is so critical to understanding the problem, leaders need to educate their subordinates concerning such biblical conflict experiences. Using these as case studies helps people learn resolution techniques without referring directly to anyone in the group. This activity is called group transferal. This process provides a non-threatening setting where people can gain insight into the causes, players, and resolutions of similar conflicts. They often see the similarity of their situation to the biblical illustration and can resolve personal conflicts without threat or injury.

Categories of expected conflict

In addition to the territories of conflict, there are five categories where leaders can expect conflict to emerge.

Intrapersonal

Intrapersonal conflicts occur within the person, or internally. They can be due to a struggle with conflicting values, expectations, or even a person's own performances. Frequently, an underlying factor prompts otherwise unexplainable conflicting behavior. The source of this conflict was explained in chapter 10 when presenting the underlying cause of all behavior. Leaders should not quickly dismiss this category as the target of their resolution technique. Very often, intrapersonal conflict actually causes interpersonal conflict.

Interpersonal

Although the word *inter*personal is very similar to the word *intra*personal, they have different meanings. Interpersonal conflict means *between* persons. Leaders often encounter this type conflict in ministry. As stated above, sometimes interpersonal conflicts are actually caused by intrapersonal conflicts. Because the interpersonal conflict is usually more visible, leaders mistakenly think the solution can be achieved by encouraging people to put away their differences and "just get along." This may not be effective, however, since often the conflict is really an intrapersonal one.

Intragroup
Again, note the prefix, *intra.* Intragroup refers to conflict that occurs within a group. Such conflict, of course, is only interpersonal conflict in a group setting. Thus, what is said above also applies to this category.

Intergroup
Intergroup conflict occurs between groups of people. Often, though, such conflict is actually between the leaders of the two groups, their spokespersons, or the persons in each group who are the most vocal. Leaders will usually find that resolving the conflict between the two group leaders will restore harmony to the groups as well.

Individual vs. the organization
In the category of individual vs. the organization conflict, it is a person and his or her opinions, values, or philosophies, which conflict with those of the entire organization.

Principles of conflict resolution
To be effective in resolving conflicts, church leaders should consider employing at least seven principles which Lewis suggests.[2] They are restated for clarity.

Help people feel good about themselves
When embroiled in conflict, many leaders feel that helping people feel good about themselves has low priority. Yet, it can be the first step to finding a redemptive resolution. An earlier chapter said that whatever people believe, they do. Following this advice, leaders should first help people feel good about themselves, then they can go on to help them resolve conflictive behaviors.

Although it may sound as if every leader must be a psychologist to resolve conflict, this, however, isn't really necessary. Leaders can help people resolve conflict by, first of all, affirming the person's worth as an individual and, second, assuring them that they can feel good about themselves even though they are involved in a conflict setting. Remember, significance and security are essential components in building self-esteem.

Insure effective communication
Nearly all conflict involves some aspect of poor communication.[3] Both verbal and written communications have their values and liabilities. Leaders should use as many approaches as possible. Feelings are not always accurately expressed in words. Leaders who employ only verbal techniques run the risk

of others forgetting the specifics of the conversation. To avoid conflict, whatever vehicle is used, always ask receivers to restate their understanding of the communication and then try to clear up any miscommunicated information together.

Clarify all assumptions

Each person comes into conflict settings with their own set of assumptions as to the facts and circumstances involved. Unfortunately, each person's assumptions may or may not be true. In every conflict situation, leaders must carefully unearth what each participant believes are the facts regarding the conflict. After hearing what each one relates, in their own words, leaders may want to express both participants' assumptions and ask them if your interpretations are correct. If not, leaders should have the participants suggest corrections. Remember that beliefs produce behaviors, which then produce feelings.

Keep true goals in sight

When conflicts arise, always keep the goals the group is trying to achieve in sight. Raising this goal afresh helps participants gain perspective concerning how the immediate conflict affects that goal achievement. Often the conflict centers around a completely different goal, perhaps a personal rather than the original group goal. Restating and reestablishing the group goal's priority can reduce the conflict intensity.[4]

Identify the real issue

When conflicts arise, the issues often get quite complex, so complex that it becomes difficult to sort out the facts involved. When this happens, take an index card and, writing on only one side of the card, try to succinctly express the real issue. In each conflict situation a myriad of side roads and tangential mountains often arise. Leaders sometimes become so embroiled in these connected issues that they fail to target the original issue which caused the conflict.

Consider alternatives to goal achievement

For the person as well as the group, arriving at the goal is usually more important than how it is achieved. Since people's personalities, temperaments, learning, behavior, and decision styles differ so widely, agreeing on how to achieve a goal is quite remote.[5] Rather than allowing the group to get bogged down with controversy on how to accomplish a goal, ask the group members for their ideas on how to achieve the goal and discuss each one. Perhaps an alternative will surface that is better than the approach under controversy.

Take a proactive stance

Leaders make a mistake when they take a reactive stance regarding conflict. That is, they respond only after conflict emerges. A better leadership tactic, however, is to be proactive in resolving conflicts. In the normal course of accomplishing tasks and before conflicts have occurred, leaders should build into their leadership style opportunities for participants to express their differing opinions, values, and interpretations.[6]

Leader response styles

Each leader will, of necessity, develop a response style to conflict. That style will impact how each conflict is resolved. Thus, that style must express biblical approaches as well as goals. In developing response styles, leaders must consider the available alternatives and approaches.[7]

Leaders have at least seven alternatives to choose from as they exercise their leadership within conflict.

Ignore the controversy

Assume that if enough time passes, the issue will resolve itself. Since people tend to drive their feelings underground when issues are not faced openly, it is not likely this will happen. Though leaders may think the issue is dead, it likely will be more intensely expressed when it surfaces again in another setting.

Stay aloof of controversy by not getting involved

Leaders often like to dream that the participants will resolve the conflict on their own. This rarely happens. Most people do not understand what truly has caused the conflict. Thus, without outside help, they are powerless to resolve the conflict.

Pretend to deal with conflict but avoid real involvement

Attempting to provide superficial solutions as a sideline coach rarely resolves conflict. Rather than wasting time with pretending to deal with the issues, leaders should use the time for sorting out, discussing, and solving the problem.

Manipulate the issue to serve the leader's goals

Some leaders use a conflict setting to promote their own agenda. Sometimes this appears to be successful, but eventually it causes participant resentment and further conflict.

Discredit the opposition

Rather than deal with the issues their opposition raised, some leaders chose to discredit their opponent. Though sometimes successful, these tactics carry negative future implications.

Suppress the conflict by wielding power and authority

Again, this method sometimes appears to be effective, but the issue will resurface elsewhere under different settings. The leader builds a "score" with his opposition that will surely emerge under other conditions.

Deal with the issue redemptively
For Christian leaders, this is really the only alternative. The following steps will help leaders to act redemptively in conflict.
- *Admit a conflict exists.* Bring it before the Lord in prayer, recognizing it is an event God expects the leader to resolve in a redemptive manner.
- *Clarify the issues involved.* Identify the real issue by stripping away the peripheral ones.
- *Gather adequate and relevant facts.* Rejecting rumor, hearsay, and suppositions, determine the facts in the case.
- *Analyze the issue.* Again, bring it before the Lord. Ask for divine wisdom and insight. Apply "what if" thinking to each facet of the issue.
- *Work to eliminate disruptive factors.* Often behavior "smokescreens" try to redirect the leader's attention to non-critical factors. Remove these factors from the setting.
- *Arrive at a constructive, redemptive conclusion.* Keep in mind that God always acts redemptively with His children. As His representative, we must do likewise.

Approaches for resolving conflicts

Though authors cite six to ten different approaches for dealing with conflict, only three are options for Christian leaders. Keep in mind, however, there are times when leaders are wise to avoid conflict—when the issue is so trivial, the confrontation so great, or the resolution so unimportant.

Win-lose approach

In the win-lose approach, either the majority, the minority, or the leader rules. Although many Christians mistakenly believe that no one should have to lose when decisions are made and conflict is resolved, it can be appropriate if group goals are achieved in a redemptive manner. Win-lose decisions can be found throughout the Bible, which God lifts up as positive models. This approach is wrong when it serves personal rather than group goals. The entire philosophy of parliamentary procedure is that of win-lose. In that win-lose, however, everyone has been treated fairly, given every chance to express dissenting opinions, and to influence the group with their viewpoint. Additionally, as mentioned above, in the Christian setting, everyone has to also have been treated redemptively.

Lose-lose approach

The lose-lose approach allows for compromise, neutral third party arbitration, or side-payments to gain acceptance. Although in this approach everyone loses something, usually what is lost is less than what is gained. Though this approach may appear to be non-Christian, it is, in fact, quite biblical. Compromise is not necessarily negative. Marriage requires compromise. Amos asks, "Do two walk together unless they have agreed to do so?" (Amos 3:3 NIV). Sometimes participants are so involved in their point of view they cannot see reality. Thus, a neutral third party helps them to find a way to agree. At other times, it may be necessary to give side-payments (promises of support, cooperation, or commitment) to one or both of the participants so that group goals can be achieved. When desireable goals are achieved and the participants are treated redemptively, lose-lose strategies can be acceptable to Christian leaders.

Win-win approach

Often thought to be the only Christian solution, the win-win approach is but one. It does, however, carry the most positive group implications. Everyone in the group, or conflict, wins. Such approaches involve collaborating, synergizing, and/or problem-solving. Collaboration suggests working together toward a common goal. Synergism suggests that a greater goal than either of the two participant's goals is found and achieved. Problem-solving lays down the group goal and enables the opposing participants to solve the problem regarding how they will achieve that goal from their personal positions.

Whichever the approach church leaders use, to assure Christian outcomes they should be sure to employ redemptive measures. Negative outcomes usually arise from abusing the approach. When leaders keep group goals as the focus and redemptive concerns for each person as their burden, any of these approaches to resolving conflicts are workable.

Summary

Although many feel church conflict results from the stress that is part of today's busy, involved society, looking into the Bible reveals that conflicts impacted even the infant church.

In church ministry, conflicts emerge in several categories— intrapersonal (within the person), interpersonal (between persons), intragroup (within a group), intergroup (between groups), and individual vs. organization.

Realizing that conflict is inevitable, leaders need to deal with it by employing a systematic, efficient process which ensures a just resolution.

Often the way leaders respond to conflict impacts how they are resolved. Leaders need to direct their involvement toward dealing with the issue redemptively.

Keeping in mind that there are times when leaders are wise to avoid conflicts—when the issue is so trivial, the confrontation so great, or the resolution so unimportant—Christians should recognize that there are three approaches for resolving conflicts: win-lose, lose-lose, and win-win.

Notes

1. Leslie B. Flynn, *Great Church Fights*, p. 9ff, Wheaton: Victor Books, 1976.
2. C. Douglass Lewis, *Resolving Church Conflicts*, p. 49-73, San Francisco: Harper and Row, 1981.
3. William M. Pinson, Jr., *How To Deal With Controversial Issues*, Nashville: Broadman Press, 1966.
4. Em Griffin, *The Mind Changers*, Wheaton: Tyndale House, 1976.
5. Phillip L. Hunsaker and Anthony J. Alessandra, *The Art of Managing People*, Englewood Cliffs, NJ: Prentice-Hall, 1980.
6. Craig S. Rice, *Getting Good People and Keeping Them*, Amacom, 1982.
7. Richard Patterson, *Creatively Resolving Church Conflicts*, Ministering with Confidence series, Wheaton: Evangelical Training Association, 1991.

For further consideration

1. Review the biblical accounts of conflicts cited at the beginning of this chapter. What insights can you draw?
2. Where would you place the power source in each of these biblical illustrations?

Application activities

1. As you reflect on your leadership role, from which category do you anticipate most of your conflicts arising?
2. In these anticipated conflicts what style do you think you will prefer for responding to them?

SHARPENING YOUR LEADERSHIP SKILLS 12

Have you ever heard someone say, "He's a born leader," or "She's a self-made woman"? Statements like these make us wonder, "Are leaders born or made?" Actually, the answer is probably both. Leaders may be born with certain genetic traits which help them to be effective. These traits, however, do not automatically make a person an effective leader. Leadership is more complex than simply having the right genetic structure. Bennis says, "Leadership is as much an art as it is a science."[1] That is, individuality is as necessary in becoming a leader as it is for a sculptor, painter, or musician. Though leadership principles can be studied, becoming an effective leader is not learned directly. Leadership is a very individualized skill.

When leadership is presented in a Christian setting, however, the spiritual gift of administration, as taught in the Bible, needs to be considered. Genetics and individual expression are still involved, but for the Christian, spiritual gifting needs to be part of the equation. Effective church leaders are not the product of proper genetics and individual charisma alone. To be effective in church leadership, people also need the call and gifting of God.

A further element in being a church leader is choice. Paul, Samson, and Shamgar are good examples of how choice contributes to effectiveness in leadership.

The apostle Paul was confronted with unchangeable factors in his life. Yet, within these parameters, Paul exercised choice and controlled change to his, and the Lord's, best interests. Paul found that though he was seized, harshly brought before the Council, and unjustly charged before Felix, Festus, and Agrippa, he had control within each structure. Paul exercised choice in a manner which positively affected change in his life.

Conversely, Samson succumbed to changes happening around him, even though he had a powerful position and was physically strong. God appointed Samson to lead, but he was a natural failure as a leader. All it took was choice.

Although less known, Shamgar also had an important leadership position. He was the third judge of Israel (Judg. 3:31). Though Shamgar did not have all the trappings of power and prestige, he used what he had—an oxgoad. With that oxgoad he slew 600 Philistines. Shamgar exercised choice, used what he had, and found that it was enough.

Church leaders today can learn three important lessons from these Bible characters. First, some change is beyond the scope of your control. Like Paul, however, you can control elements within these unchangeable factors to positively impact your world. Second, though you hold an impressive church office, through the careless choice of inaction, like Samson you can lose your ability to effect change in your world. Or, third, like Shamgar, by depending on the Lord for results, you can effect important changes by using whatever you have, regardless of how humble.

Church leaders can sharpen their leadership skills by using these four principles: depend upon your call to leadership, develop others through delegation, deepen yourself through continuing education, and determine to be God's change agent.[2] The following sections will consider each of these principles in more detail.

Depend upon your call to leadership

According to Habecker, no church leader should be, "In a position of leadership without a clear sense from the Lord that he or she is God's choice for that position."[3] Sadly, such personal assessments are often uncommon in the church. Rather than sensing a clear call from God, far too often church leaders attribute their positions to elections, appointments, and volunteerism. Undoubtedly this is why church leadership is at such an all-time low today. Many of those serving in typical local church leadership positions have romantically reserved God's call only to missionaries and senior pastors. Nothing could be further from biblical truth.

Church leaders can never hope to be effective in God's eyes if they see their role as the consequence only of successful candidating and politicking. Neither will these leaders ever hope to feel a sense of accomplishment or fulfillment in their leadership roles.

Understand that the burden of leadership is the Lord's

With the sharpening of leaders' realizations that they are called of God for leadership in the church comes a heavy burden. In an earlier chapter, that burden was exemplified in Moses' life in the events in Exodus 18. With increasing frequency, the results of that burden also cause today's church leaders to experience "brownout, burnout, and bow out." The personal weight caused by having more tasks than time, more complaints than praises, and more goats than sheep, can be an overwhelming burden.

Church leaders, however, need to learn a lesson from the life of Gideon. He had a call from God and a task to perform for Him, but the burden of that task was enormous. Gideon was to go to war against incredible odds. The Lord wanted to show Gideon, however, that the burden really was His. Thus, He told Gideon to reduce his army! In so doing, God wanted to increase the odds against Gideon's winning. It would seem that God was increasing Gideon's burden. The Bible, however, reveals something else. In Judges 7:2, God says, "The people who are with you are too many *for Me to give Midian* into their hands, lest Israel become boastful, saying, 'My own power has delivered me'" (italic added). What God asked Gideon to do was His burden to accomplish, not Gideon's. In assuming that burden, God also expected the glory for the outcome. Habecker says of this passage, "As leaders we are tempted to give Him the burdens and then claim the glory. God wants both the burdens and the glory."[4] The church leader's burden of ministry is actually the Lord's burden.

Appreciate that vision is the key

An important difference between leaders and followers is vision. Most effective leaders have it, followers often lack it. Vision is the ability to see environmental circumstances in a critical light, manifest a deep dissatisfaction with what is, while envisioning what could be. The essense of vision is "being effective as opposed to being efficient." Vision is the leader's exclusive domain. No one else is charged with such a task. Sadly, many leaders, especially in the lower ranks of church leadership, push that task to the higher ranks of leadership. Confronted by the tyranny of the urgent, many upper echelon leaders default on vision. The sad result is that the church, department, program, or unit, flounders for lack of direction.

Develop others through delegation

Looking again at Moses, in Numbers 11:16,17 God instructs and advises him to delegate some of his leadership tasks to others. "The Lord therefore said to Moses, 'Gather for Me seventy men from the elders of Israel, whom you know to be the elders of the people and their officers and bring them to the tent of meeting and let them take their stand there with you. Then I will come down and speak with you there, and I will take of the Spirit who is upon you, and will put Him upon them; and they shall bear the burden of the people with you, so that you shall not bear it all alone.'"

Some church leaders prefer not to delegate any of their power to others. They argue they want all of the Spirit's power, not a portion. Yet, the Bible does not teach that the Spirit's power was diminished upon Moses or any other leader who delegated. In fact, it could be argued that through delegation Moses actually had more of the Spirit's power concentrated upon his leadership than before he delegated (his plus his delegates).

Conger's research of the most successful leaders revealed that they "empowered others to achieve the dream." He defines empowerment as "essentially a process of strengthening subordinate's convictions in their own self-efficacy." Different from simply delegating power to a subordinate, empowerment taps the motivational energy of subordinates toward achieving goals the leader has selected. Conger cites four sources for developing this empowerment among subordinates. They are: positive task accomplishment, verbal encouragement, stirring of positive emotions, and modeling outcomes.[5]

Positive task accomplishment

The first, and most basic, step is delegating achievable tasks to subordinates which are likely to be accomplished satisfactorily. As subordinates sense they can accomplish such delegated tasks, they are more willing to take on greater and more complex responsibilities. Positive, rather than negative, experiences with delegated tasks are essential in motivating subordinates to accomplish greater things.

Verbal encouragement

One of the most essential elements in motivating subordinates is personal approval of the leader. Leaders can express verbal encouragement in many creative ways. They are only limited by their creativity and budget.

Stirring of positive emotions

Feelings are a driving force for motivation. When subordinates feel good about their role under your leadership and the goals they are achieving as a group, they generate strong motivational power. Thus, leaders who create settings, such as recognition dinners, personal letters, recognition gifts, etc., reinforce and empower their delegation to their subordinates.

Modeling outcomes

Leaders are models for the subordinates. They are the visible symbol of the group's mission. Subordinates believe that leaders know what it takes to achieve the group's goals. Subordinates watch their leaders carefully for clues to successful accomplishment of tasks. Therefore, leaders must be sufficiently visible to the subordinates. This may mean they should perform tasks alongside subordinates to insure they recognize a good model.

Deepen yourself through continuing education

Leaders must make long-range plans for continuing their own equipping and training. It is quite possible that, when the Lord chose you for a lay leadership role, it was but a first step in His ultimate plan. Many Sunday school superintendents or church board members have later become pastors, Bible college instructors, seminary professors, or Christian organizational executives. Two principles are important in working toward this goal.

Operate from an agenda

An agenda is a plan of action. Establish an agenda for each day. Place tasks that are of greatest priority at the top, then work through each one. Writing the tasks on a daily personal calendar is often helpful in organizing them. Then as each task is completed, check it off the list.

While short-term exercises can be listed on the personal calendar, long-term plans need to be handled differently. Researching educational opportunities is an ongoing task for the growing leader. These might include correspondence courses or college extension courses. Continuing education opportunities for the Christian leader are readily available today. Leaders must determine in what areas they need the most help and begin to create an agenda for completing this training.

Given the amount of change leaders face in churches today, each leader should be taking at least one course a year for further development.

In addition, leaders should be purchasing and reading good books to help them to develop. Try to purchase at least two books each year. Often church budgets allow for such purchases. Similarly, leaders should subscribe to periodicals that will keep them abreast of leadership issues.

Be open to other leadership tasks

Experience helps church leaders become more successful. Therefore, leaders ought to accept tasks that will help them broaden and mature their leadership capabilities. Starting at the bottom and working your way up is sound advice for all leaders. Nothing can be more overwhelming than to be placed in a leadership role beyond your capabilities. The "Peter Principle" says that all leaders will eventually rise to their level of incompetency. That is, as people do well in lesser leadership roles, they are often promoted to more powerful leadership levels. At some point, the principle states, these leaders will be promoted beyond their abilities. It is sad that this happens quite often.

Such need not be the experience of Christian leaders if they are careful to establish continuing education agendas and are willing to gain experience in accepting a wide array of leadership tasks.

Determine to be God's change agent

Change is happening more rapidly than ever before in history. Change has the church and its leadership under great stress. Which way to go? Which advice to follow? What programs to adopt? Which ones to terminate? Leaders are constantly dealing with change questions like these. Given today's society, changes will continue to accelerate. Change, then, is the setting in which church leaders find themselves. Such change should not be resisted, but used for the glory of God. Thus, church leaders have no other choice but to accept the role of change agents. It is and has always been the model of all God's leaders.

Schaller observes, "That by action or inaction every person does influence the future." Further, he says, "The person who has a systematic approach to the future and a frame of reference for evaluating alternatives has a tremendous advantage over the person who functions without either."[6] Thus, whether leaders choose to serve as change agents or not, they still influence the future—rightly or wrongly. Having a systematic approach to effecting change gives leaders great advantage in achieving goals for God.

Knowing and following the five principles presented below will help leaders effect change.

Raise the level of discontent

The first step to effecting change is raising the level of discontent. This might sound unchristian, but it is nonetheless true. As long as people are satisfied in the circumstances around them, they are not motivated to make changes. Just as the definition of having vision was "the ability to be dissatisfied with conditions as they now are and visualize what could be done to make those conditions better," so also is the definition of the change agent.

The principle is not that leaders should create discontent among the members of the church. Rather, it is that leaders should take the discontent that already exists concerning a circumstance, issue, thing, or person, and raise it to a higher consciousness level of those involved.

Develop a group to identify areas needing change

The leader does not want all changes to be perceived as a personal quest. It must become a group quest. Therefore, leaders need to identify those persons in the larger group who carry power of the types described in chapter 9. Remember these people will likely hold informal, not formal power. They will be those who begin to sow further seeds of discontent regarding the issue. These people, however, need to be seen by the larger group as credible persuaders. This initiatory group owns the discontent and seeks to get others to join them.

Identify the forces perpetuating the problem

In order to develop a change strategy, the leader needs to identify and fully understand the issue that has caused the discontent. Reviewing chapter 11 will help in this area.

Devise a strategy to effect change

The church leader's role in the change setting is devising a strategy for effecting the change. The leader has the vision of what should come from changing this circumstance, issue, event, person, or thing. The leader will devise steps to guide the group toward a problem-solving attitude which will result in acceptable change.

Nurture the support group

As the initiatory group grows to include sufficient numbers, the leader can then consider it a support group for the change. These people need to have influence with the remaining group. As the discontent continues to be nurtured, increasing numbers of persons will join the support group.

As with many situations, people will react to change in a variety of ways. It will help the leader to know that in every group there are certain percentages of people who respond to change in predictable ways. The five basic ways people respond to change are:

Early innovators—They represent about 7% of the group. They jump on the bandwagon almost immediately. From this group the leader can create the initiatory group.

Early adopters—Coming a little later in the change sequence, these people represent about 15% of the group. They form the nurture group described above.

Show-mes—Joining the nurture group somewhat later is this group of about 30%.

Tag-alongs—Once the majority of the group has begun to swing in a specified direction, this group is willing to tag-along. They represent about 38%.

Non-adopters—These people only constitute about 10% of the total group.

Leaders can see that at the outset of encouraging change, they will find that only 7% of the people desire it. This should not discourage leaders from becoming change agents. Soon another 15% will join the movement. While in the heat of the discussion for change, another 30% will join. At that point, leaders have over one-half (52%) of the group seeking change. Continuing with this change strategy will lead another 38% to accept the change.

Summary

Each church leader has a choice to make concerning how to sharpen their leadership skills. Like Samson, God will allow them to neglect their leadership gifts. Though the burden of leadership is heavy, that burden, as well as the glory of accomplishment, belongs to the Lord. Leaders serve in stewardship capacities. Leaders are also the only persons to whom God gives vision. Such vision, however, must be exercised in methodical ways to effect change for the better.

Finally, the leaders' successes depend not only upon relying on the Lord for wisdom and power, but also upon empowering their ministry teams. All of these elements must be honed and sharpened in a systematic fashion if they are to realize that coveted phrase, "Well done, good and faithful servant" (Matt. 25:21 NIV). As Greenslade tells us, "It is an enormous privilege for any leader to be caught up in the same movement of divine grace that brought the Son of God into the world."[7]

Notes
1. Warren Bennis, *Why Leaders Can't Lead*, p. 145.
2. Richard Patterson, *Developing Church Leaders*, Ministering with Confidence series, Wheaton: Evangelical Training Association, 1991.
3. Eugene B. Habecker, *The Other Side of Leadership*, p. 60-72.
4. *ibid.*
5. Jay A. Conger, *The Charismatic Leader*, p. 107ff.
6. Lyle E. Schaller, *The Change Agent*, p. 78-120.
7. Philip Greenslade, *Leadership, Greatness, and Servanthood*, p. 121, Minneapolis, MN: Bethany House, 1984.

For further consideration
1. What are the three leadership lessons which can be learned from Paul, Samson, and Shamgar?
2. Of the four principles presented in this chapter, in which one are you the strongest? In which are you the weakest? What steps can you take to improve?
3. List the things you as a leader currently do as recognition for your subordinates. What others could you add to encourage your subordinates and enhance their motivation?
4. Are you and your church in a position to effect change for God? Develop a strategy, using the principles for effecting change, that will put you and your church in a place where positive change can be made according to God's plan.

Application activities
1. Study strong biblical leadership figures for consequences of the choices they made which affected their leadership (for example, Solomon's choice of wives, etc.).
2. Develop short and long range plans for enhancing your gifts and training in leadership. Write it as a personal agenda with dates for completion.